A Life Worth Living - A Story Worth Telling

Morgan Scott Phenix

ISBN: 1492172278

ISBN 13: 9781492172277

$\mathcal{M}$ E N U

Oh that my words were now written!
Oh that they were printed in a book!

JOB 19:23 KJV

To the untold stories:

may they flow from your heart,

and be told in print.

WHAT HAPPENED

The life. The story. They crossed paths at a community college in Virginia, two years after I retired as high school principal in the Shenandoah Valley. Retired and tired. I became dean for humanities, math and social sciences at Lord Fairfax Community College, about an hour's drive north from home, up the interstate. Two or more hours a day, sapping my resolve, but adding to the conversations in my head, the questions, the ideas, the too many what-ifs from a lifetime that seemed to be closing down.

The Story. One of my English faculty, Professor Brent Kendrick, former Library of Congress researcher, asked about offering a course in memoir writing.

"Yes. Of course," I said. He was a remarkable instructor, and the students would get a special opportunity if they were looking outside the ordinary.

He asked, "Why don't you take it, boss?"

I told him the class probably wouldn't make, for lack of enrollment, but added, "OK, I'll sign on if it goes." It made.

Two years later, having also approved Memoir Writing II and Creative Nonfiction I and II, I sat in the last of the four classes I had approved and signed up for; I was ready to retire for good. I felt that I had nothing left to say, having written for the classes over one hundred pieces of life's history, reflection, dreams, regrets and apologies. But I knew at that point that I would publish something (see *Meeting Ivory Rose*). The Good Professor had a syllabus, but allowed us to propose a project in line with our special interests. A perfect chance to arrange all the pieces I had written over four semesters, craft a few chronological tabs to set them apart, and here it is. *A Life Worth Living. A Story Worth Telling.*

The Life. The Story. The title is presumptuous: "a life worth living"— as if some life might not be. And almost arrogant—"a story worth telling"—as if some, or most, are not. But, truth be told, most stories are only imagined or dreamed, or remembered only in the hearts of the closest loved ones. Most stories contain enough chagrin and boredom and regret to slow any wish or plan to tell all.

The Story: nearing the end of my working life, and with sights set on the question marks of old age, I chose to gather together all the hundred-plus pieces of fact and fancy that I had written for the professor's classes. Not as an autobiography or journal or memoir. Simply an ending to my gathering, and an invitation to yours. It's an invitation to use this moment in time—all we have, really—to share the snapshots of a lifetime, before it's too late; to try to find some of the separate threads that create the firm fabric of a life. And perhaps arrive at a revelation or two, about what was most important, most treasured, most neglected, most critical.

The Life: Just yesterday (as I write these words), just yesterday, crossing the Alma Bridge west of Stanley, hot summer day, I passed a half-coiled black snake in the middle of the road. He had been hit, grievously, and was twisting in a futile attempt to angle his way off the hot road, to safety, home. His final agony welled up in me. The essence of life. Angling toward the cooler edge of the road, toward life, no guardian near enough to rescue or save. I am simply filled with the rush and essence of life. Just life.

ACKNOWLEDGING MY DEBT

First, Professor of English Brent Kendrick at Lord Fairfax Community College in Middletown, Virginia who demonstrated the hunger in many hearts to write memoir and creative nonfiction; and to the college, for allowing me to take part. I note the first writing assignments: five-hundred-word essays in the style of NPR's *This I Believe,* and Natalie Goldberg's* *Take Ten* exercises, constructions clearly identifiable in this book.

Second, loving and strained memories of Philip Henry Phenix, my father, and Gena Tenney Phenix, my mother, who allowed my brother and me tremendous freedom. Also, gentler thanks for Dr. John (Jack) and Helene MacConnell, who served as beloved dad and mom over thirty years of my life.

Brother, Roger Branscombe Phenix, who tends the Tenney family archives and memories at his Stony Point, New York house in the woods. Roger was my childhood hero, beginning his odyssey into film with his camera purchase at age five; his understanding of documentary provided key checkpoints for organizing this book. The John Manning photo was his unexpected and priceless gift to me.

Sheena Lynn Palmer, brilliant overachieving daughter, for companionship and encouragement over many years, particularly into retirement, for her wistful and beautiful front and back cover design for this book.

Betty Housden Phenix, companion, wife, and friend for more than twenty years. I am still here. Meanda Love Housden, daughter, who delivered Bianca into this world, a gift, the only child I've known since a baby, my *Little Red*.

Page County; George School; Denmark; Muhlenberg College; Milwaukee: all grassy slopes yielding especially awkward bouquets of flowers.

Ivory Rose, for permission to publish her *Torn Dreams* cover art.

The grace of God, His perfect Word, and Jesus' companionship on the road...

*Goldberg, Natalie. *Old Friend from Far Away: The Practice of Writing Memoir*. New York: Free Press. 2007. Print

A Story Worth Telling—The Idea

June, 2012: He is so persistent. The persistent professor, in the office smiling, pacing, excited, telling about plans for the next course in his memoir sequence. I've taken the first three and don't believe there's anything else to say. I'm done. Plus, I'm retiring from the college.

He says, "Creative Nonfiction II, to round things out." I'm in his current class, and we're winding down to the finish of Creative Nonfiction I. He is pacing and already excited about the next class. "At least eight have already said they'll be there."

I thought, *No, I'm tired and I'm struggling with the drive up the interstate. And more than that, I am worried about my energy, my plan, my memory, what I'm going to do next.* But mainly, I was just tired.

I said, "Remember, this is my last week on campus. I'm retired in a week. Next week." Retired, but mostly just tired.

"It's going to be a hybrid. Only meet a handful of times. We'll talk about it." Out the door he goes, pure energy, optimism, and a dazzling ability to chide and hustle and move people forward, even when they don't want to budge. I was tired. I am tired. Amazing. The professor and I were about the same age.

I hadn't told the professor about what had happened as I began to put together my portfolio of pieces from the current class. I had turned

1

back to my Memoir II class files, to find for comparison an introductory statement I had done, and in the process wandered around in the nearly one hundred short biographical essays I had written. There were more than a few that I didn't fully recognize. I did not recall thinking about the subject, only vaguely understood that I had in fact written them. Snapshots of my life, brief encounters with other times and places and persons, and I had to struggle to recollect the subject or even the occasion for touching on it. For a class only a half a year before.

I was overwhelmed as well at the notion of losing the files, a house fire or flood or catastrophe, never being able to re-create or even recall the material. If I ever wanted to write a memoir, how could I find the energy or the will? Simply the overwhelming mass of words. This was part of my daily fatigue, that the beauty and adventure and value of days gone by could never be revisited without wellsprings of energy and insight that I now truly lacked. At this point in my life. At this retiring point in my life. Retreating. And the professor's accusing courses, which ultimately asked about the worth of the life, or at least the worth of the story. A story worth telling?

I am convinced that my situation, my state of mind, my fears and fatigue, as a sixty-six-year-old retiring community college administrator, are not uncommon. I am convinced that there are thousands, perhaps millions, of precious souls weighing past against future and wondering about the life worth living, the story worth telling, and increasingly unsure that it could ever be recalled, revisited, let alone recounted.

Likewise, my one-hundred-plus sketches about days and years lived out at full speed, in full knowledge and intent, splashes of color and voice and emotion, are unique to my own time alive, yet I am certain they are reflected in any other person's encounter with the past and with memory, and everything that attaches to that journey of recall and rendering: thanksgiving, regret, pride, shame, pain, joy, and more.

I signed up for the class, retired from the college, drove home, and put the matter out of my mind. I had written no creative words really, not ever, other than one or two things in high school and in college composition classes, but nothing else until the memoir series with the professor, over two years' time, so late in this life. Yet I know clearly that I have verbalized and conceptualized and romanticized my existence at every turn, over the decades of travel and study, work, marriages, adventures. Plenty to write about in the classes.

It was truly all about me, always, and so, almost as a mocking and knowing poke at my predicament, during the second meeting of the new class, a film clip warning from a professional memoirist: that to rise above journal writing, passing along day-by-day quips on what happened, there had to be a story line, a thread, a binding theme, a purpose leading toward resolution, forward to final settlement, relief, understanding. Toward what makes a story worth telling.

OK, then, here we are, for today. Since my energy is fleeting, my memory faltering, I will draw the pieces together and arrange them within a storyboard. But the central investigation will be to find the theme that draws it all together, not necessarily along the way, but in the end. There are several pieces that I have not written, have not even touched upon in my heart, that might describe the all-encompassing journey, no, the quest, the odyssey, that leads me home, settling, at peace. Wish us well.

A STORY WORTH TELLING—BEING BORN

And deliver them who through fear of death were all their lifetime subject to bondage. HEB 2:15 KJV

I do not remember being born, though I recall waking nightmares as a very young child. Nightmares whose terror was so generalized, yet tangible, could only have come from revisiting, in fevered dreams, such trauma as one must encounter entering this world. The same nightmare, and screams that neighbors described as a cat howling, recurred for years, whenever I was hit with high temperature, colds, or flu. Terror. A dividing line between death and life, or life and nothingness and back.

I remember even earlier, my mother sitting on my bedside, nighttime, asking me as a four-year-old why I didn't want to go with them to church. And I clearly remember telling her that it was "because Jesus makes you die." And only now, six decades later, do I begin to recognize a consistent story line, a true pattern, that runs parallel to the unfolding hodgepodge events of my experience, which I will shortly begin to unburden.

I have a desktop screensaver photo slide show that places the image of a high school friend, Hollister, in front of me daily in thirty-second flashes, inviting me to recall and question and organize the tragic chronology surrounding his death nearly fifty years ago. He's standing at attention, military, beside his old Hillman Minx, and the car is lined up nose to nose with old tractor trailers at a truck stop, in Ohio or Indiana. We drove to Minnesota to see my old hometown, Northfield, over Christmas vacation, 1963. Hollister is staring straight ahead. Was he thinking *firing squad*, maybe?

Hollister, after a failed attempt by auto crash, with broken collar bone and bed-ridden, killed himself using the very gun they told us his grandfather had used to end his own life. I realized Hollister's story line swung around the axle of wanting to die. *Wanting to die*, I thought. *How could a person want to die?* But it seemed like that was what he actually was trying to do all along the way, acting crazy and manic, shouting and laughing, just acting crazy.

And now, just as I write these words, remembering us speeding in his dad's car, passing a line of stopped double-lane highway traffic on the right-hand gravel shoulder of the road at sixty miles an hour, Sunday evening ride back from Ocean City, to Pennsylvania. Hollister's dad's convertible Ford Fairlane, four boys shouting, laughing, cheating death. But we didn't know then what it was, that Hollister might have actually wanted to die. We just figured he was crazy, just a little more than we were. Dave Hollister was my good friend, and his story line wish was the flip side of my own.

In the professor's writing class, I listened to an expert describe the difference between journal and authentic memoir, the one being a chronology of days and people and things that happened, maybe with some fleeting thoughts attached, the other an unfolding of a life's story spun around patterns of meaning toward a purpose or a climax or a tragedy, but in any case a resolution. Of a story. A Story.

I was shocked to arrive at the point of recognition that brings clarity to chaos. The central theme of Hollister's story is tragic, and consistent. And so is mine. His story is all about a desire to die, but my story springs from, and is fed by, the agonized demand that I live forever. All the journal entries of my life, every plan, every dream, every trip, every study or work or engagement or marriage, every act of kindness, every crime, every prayer, every lie, every grasp in the night, has been in service of my own central theme: that I live forever, that I not die, that I not return to nothingness.

I have an excuse; perhaps this is a baby boomer thing. Perhaps it's all about that 1940s pool of wandering and terrified souls set loose in blitzkriegs and death camps, vaporized in atomic firestorms, starved in ice and winter, returned to a dazzling age of possibility, of promise, of growth and guarantee. We are one hundred million souls in this country alone, a billion more around the world watching and wanting the same, but suddenly moving toward the end of time, all at once too many to count or feed or even imagine. We were born to unbridled potentiality, no challenge too daunting, no horizon too far, no question unanswered, no heresy or outrage or deviance too extreme.

So, after a half century of accumulated events and happenings, places we've been and seen and left and revisited, we need a story. We need a story. And we need the resolution, to turn one thing and another, here and there, this and that, into a poem, a tale, a portrait, a gift. We need the opportunity to draw together the bits and pieces of our lives, the details we can remember and dare divulge, and recreate them as a story worth telling. A story worth telling, so that the end, the eventual recognition, the drawing together, satisfies and justifies both the journey and the telling. A story worth telling.

If this story is not worth telling, so be it. I am going to write it and print it, regardless. That's another story in itself, about the threat and promise to tell, simply tell; that's coming too. And between just you and me, I'll bet there are a million other people who would love to do just the same. Or ten million perhaps, or a hundred million. Or perhaps it is part of God's plan, that each and every last one of us should have a story worth telling. Perhaps each and every last one, called to resolution, to judgment.

ON KINDNESS
"THANK YOU, MOTHER"

"Bianca, you've got to go out to the car with your little friend and thank her mom for letting her stay over."

"Daddy, why?" Impatient, cross face, a regular scene, but she goes.

I walk to the door and call to Holly's mom, "Holly's always welcome. Thanks for letting her stay over. She's the greatest!"

Bianca sulks in. "I don't know why I have to do that, and I was telling her anyway, and then you had to say all that stuff!"

I remember Mother and try to recall the familiar frustration of my childhood, so often failing in that simple act of thanking someone for a kindness.

I walk home from Bessa Rayment's birthday party. She's my first grade friend. But the contentment of that afternoon evaporates as I meet Mother at our back door. "How was the party?"

"Good." Knowing certainly what's coming next. And that I have forgotten.

"Scottie, did you thank Mrs. Rayment? For the party?" I hesitate only the slightest moment, but it's too late, and Mother knows, as if she had spoken with Bessa's mom. "Wait while I get my coat. I'll go with you."

"Mother, I'm sure I said thank you!"

"Then let's thank her again." And we walk. Three blocks, silent. Crisp Minnesota air. Mrs. Rayment listens as my mother introduces my return visit. "Scottie has something to say."

"Thank you for the party, Mrs. Rayment. It was really nice."

I remember again, 1951, Saturday morning. The old Woodward couple next door invite me in to watch television for the first time in my life. A space adventure for young kids. I am captivated. I don't know what a commercial is, but Mr. Woodward copies an address to send for a plastic rocket: flying to the moon, ten cents and a cereal box top. I run home and tell Mother about the television and the rocket and the moon and the box top.

"Yes, I thanked them, Mother." And I had. "And they invited me to come back next Saturday!"

I remember. I practice so carefully what Mother teaches me that day, as if my very happiness depends on it. I practice my concern and care, my thanks and consideration. My happiness and a plastic rocket to the moon hang in the balance.

"Is it convenient for me to come in?" From the mouth of a five-year old, it must sound implausible, scripted. Old Mr. Woodward, raised eyebrows, lets me in. A key to the treasure.

"Is it convenient for me to come in?"

"Thank you very much, Mr. and Mrs. Woodward."

"Thank you, Mom."

Mom is gone, but even at ninety-five, to her I was still Scottie, and she still asked those probing, accusing questions about common kindness. Not about manners. This was about obligation and honor and opportunity, about moments not to be squandered or ignored. No allowance for carelessness or impatience or selfishness when extending kindness.

Thank you, Mom. I too believe kindness is an obligation and an honor and an opportunity.

$\mathcal{F}$ L A S H B A C K

I remember it all so clearly, once I turn the pages back. So often, it's shame or uneasiness or regret or just something lost. Last night I turned back a page, visiting the street where I had worked for three years, the apartment complex where I had lived. They both looked shabby, run-down, cold, and colorless. It was a view from Google Earth, and suddenly I did not want to visit or flee from today into yesterday. And I recall so many other times when an actual visit to the past resulted not in joyous rediscovery, but in impatience and a desire to move on.

My memories are less fond than sad. I regret the passing of years, and my own eventual passing from the scene. I consider my child Bianca's impatience with me and my nervous insistence on her behavior. She will remember how uncomfortable it was to be in our house, how demand-ing, and will not know the sentimental treasures I hold of my earlier years, which were, at the time, so full of pain and impatience, like hers.

I need to draw my years together, and to a close, so that I can enjoy a period of accepting rest, of joy in being alive, of easy breathing without distraction or demand. I need to bring things to a conclusion and to a corporate whole. Then I believe I can rest without worry or regret or as-piration or fear. To reach this point, I will write until nothing more flows, until all the stories have been told, all the grievances aired.

$\mathcal{F}$ATHER'S $\mathcal{D}$RESSER

My father's dresser-top was clean, orderly, and it was a high-boy, so we couldn't really see what was up there when it mattered most, as kids. But we knew what was there: a silver pen, or a mechanical pencil, and his pocket watch on a chain, and perhaps some loose change in a small dish. He taught at the college, or was chaplain, and he was up early every morning, writing in his study at the front of the house. He was a creature of habit and regular schedule. He kept his other important items in the top half-drawer: hairbrush, pocket calendar book, probably paper clips and a handkerchief or two. The dresser was light brown, almost red, tiger maple. The legs were slender, maybe a foot long, fluted, and the dresser had five or six full drawers and the two half-drawers, side by side at the top. The drawer pulls were hinged on flat eagle mountings, and the most distinctive feature of my father's dresser was the sound of the door pulls when he closed the drawers or let the pulls loose. A quick metallic clatter, maybe three bouncing clacks. It was a morning sound, as he prepared for the day, or an evening one as he got ready for bed.

My father was clean and spare, thin and wiry. He was a lightweight six feet tall—only slightly taller than the dresser, from our vantage point. Years later, when my father moved to the nursing home, then to our house, my brother took the dresser. My father had painted it antique white and ruined its value. The drawer pulls still clacked, two or three times, when the drawer was pushed shut.

Mother's Jewelry

It cost thirty-five cents. It's in the glass-front case, and I bought it for her in 1954 or 1955. A bow with forty or fifty light purple stones, perhaps amethyst, more likely glass. It was on the table in the Presbyterian Church bazaar before Christmas, and I bought it for Mother as a present. This piece of jewelry was the only one I ever noticed her wear, besides her tiny diamond engagement ring. Several of the stones have fallen out, and I asked a jeweler once if he could replace them. He said it would be costly to match, even though it was inexpensive costume jewelry. I found a piece very much like it when Mother lived in our home in the years leading up to her death, but when she received it, she was only polite. The purple bow is one of a kind, and it was from the years when giving first became a conscious act. That one could give an object to please another.

I bought a necklace for Connie Olsen in seventh grade, first girl I ever kissed, though I didn't really want to. But buying the necklace was an awesome adventure: choosing, and wrapping, and delivering, a note to match. An expression of care. The purple bow was bought in an instant, no agonizing or choosing. It was the right thing, cost the same as something that might mean a great deal to me, and produced a joyful reaction. A bow. The tied knot, colorful and decorative, securing the act of giving. My mother's precious gift.

15

RESTLESS—TRAVELS WITH FATHER

I learned while still relatively young, perhaps seven or eight, that when we loaded up the car and drove—when we moved—it was because something went wrong with my father's work or writing, or because he simply got a whole new plan for his life, or because he had settled on returning to a place previously abandoned. But I remember each and every place along the way, from the time I was two or three years old.

1946: I was born in New York City, and we moved in with father's parents in Montclair, New Jersey. My father served in the army and air force during the war and had plans to do graduate study and teach at Columbia. His mother, Bessie, died that year or the next, and I do not remember her, despite a comfortable photo of her holding me in her arms. I do not remember the first move to Minnesota, when father first became chaplain at Carleton College, in Northfield.

1948: We live on First Street in Northfield, Minnesota. The yard is small, both in front of the house and the backyard, flat, and the grass is pale green in summer heat, cut very short. Father pushes the lawn mower, I am sitting on the ground, and Roger is crying about something a neighbor boy has done or said. I remember the grass and the confrontation, the small flatness of the yard, and the heat.

1948: We live at 100 Claremont Avenue, New York City. Outside the window, in the street below, a garbage truck races its engine to power the hydraulic loader and compactor and we throw our toys onto the floor, climb over the edge of the wooden bed, and heave them back onto the mattress, shouting "Garbing, garbing!" I remember the noise, the toys, the bed, and my brother. Father lectures in philosophy at Columbia and is doing graduate study.

1949: We live in Shanks Village, New York. Don Richie, one of Father's friends, throws a ball into the air, to the moon, and it's out of sight, gone. We are standing on a concrete parking pad, looking up. I remember catching Mr. Richie holding the ball behind his back, never having thrown it at all. Our two-wheeled trailer is on the concrete square, waiting to be loaded with things, to move. Father is returning to Carleton College as chaplain and teaching faculty. Grandmother Tenney visits, takes us to the five-and-dime store, and we buy a small plastic toy. Mother takes us to the chicken farm, and we throw eggshells over the fence; the smell of the farm is sweet, never forgotten. My brother and I play in the "frog grass" by the creek behind the house. I remember the coarse grass, clearly.

1950: We live at 314 East Second Street, Northfield, Minnesota. The house is large, yellow-white stucco, raised on a two-foot grass embankment surrounding it on three sides, a concrete driveway on the garage side. We live on the first floor. Winters, road graders plow mountains of snow from the street, and we dig tunnels through to the street. It is cold walking to the elementary school, and there is the smell of wet mittens and snow gear drying on the radiator. I remember the kindergarten green circle on the wooden floor. Also, a horse-drawn tinker's wagon on our street, offers to sharpen scissors, fix pots and pans. Comfortable. Father writes his first book, *Intelligible Religion*, to scoffing reviews, and he leaves teaching and Carleton's chaplaincy. We pack the 1941 two-door maroon Plymouth with everything, two Siamese cats on the rear window ledge, and drive east.

1952: We live on Vineyard Road, Hamden, Connecticut. Tension. Mother travels ahead and arranges the purchase of a house, brand-new, more than we can afford. Roger and I sit in silence, and we understand that Father's new boss at the Hazen Foundation has covered the house payments. Our house on Vineyard Road is miles from the elementary school, and we take a school bus, a new and tiring experience. I do not remember my second-grade teacher. There are five apple trees in the sunny field behind our house, cool, dark woods beyond, and our female Siamese cat dies at the vet's office where Mother has taken it for spaying. Mother is convinced the vet has stolen the cat, to breed it. Father plans to return to Columbia to teach, and we leave the male cat with the house's new owners.

1953: We live at 136 High Street, Leonia, New Jersey. We live in a rented house for three months and then move several blocks to the small, two-story frame house on High Street, a quiet neighborhood full of kids on bikes and roller skates, shouts and running. My brother Roger has a paper route and buys an expensive camera. His professional life begins here. I dream of trucks and begin to cook, taking pictures of meals I've made, trying to catch up with Roger's natural talents. I learn to play the piano and boogie woogie from Larry Cremin, Father's boss at Columbia. Roger and I have many friends, play ball until too dark to see, race on bicycles, and join clubs and sports teams. Father has a minor accident in the City with the 1941 Plymouth, and we buy a new 1957 Chevrolet, larkspur blue. Larkspur blue. Thirteen, Roger falls in love with a tall, pretty girl with braids across the street at the same time we learn we're going to move back to Northfield, where Father will be dean at Carleton College. He has written a solid college textbook: *Philosophy of Education*.

1958: Madison, Wisconsin. We live in a borrowed house for several months, as Father has a teaching assignment at the University of Wisconsin. It is a barren and hot summer of boredom and loneliness. Mother arranges for a man to come and give Roger and me weight-lifting workouts, and I recall clearly I did not know why. I knew that I was athletic enough for a twelve-year-old. But I was not very assertive.

1958: We live at 314 East Second Street in Northfield, for the second time. We return to the same faculty housing at Carleton, first floor of the big stucco house, and I make friends with Jimmy Nelson, upstairs family; we are both wary of the strange professor living in the third-floor attic apartment. Roger and I begin calling Father by his new, important title, "Dean." The junior-senior high school is a block away, and everything is perfect, including canoeing and summer camp along the Gunflint Trail area, running track, building go-carts and scooters, driving a tractor on a friend's family farm, having older friends with cars and pickup trucks, and briefly, I have a girlfriend. Roger takes serious interest in guitar and folk music, while I continue with boogie and jazz piano. But after a year, Father feels he is not cut out for the personnel side of the deanship, and he will move back to Columbia. Roger reports hearing my mother suggest to Father that the family split for Roger's and my sake. My new girlfriend's father dies in his sleep, and her mother makes plans to move to California. We have a professional mover load our belongings, and we drive east. We continue to call Father "Dean," though he asks us to call him by his given name, Phil, since we are getting older: teens.

1960: We live at 501 West 120th Street, New York City. We are three blocks from Claremont Avenue, where we started. My father is at the same job he has held twice before. The move from rural Northfield to big-city New York is assumed more than two teenage boys can manage, so Roger and I go to boarding schools in Pennsylvania—Roger to Westtown School, and I to George School. The schools are co-ed Quaker schools near Philadelphia. Roger continues with his music, becomes a quiet thinker and war protester, and ultimately a conscientious objector; I run cross-country and track, play piano, and spend time with my new friends, away from the family.

1964: Postscript. Roger enters Antioch College and continues there for two years. He completes his conscientious objector assignment and goes into full-time work in film production, settling in Rockland County outside New York City. He rarely visits family. I go to the University of North Carolina at Chapel Hill and drop out in March of my freshman year, load up my motorcycle with all my things, and return to New York City. I move in with my parents and take a job with US Steel in the financial district.

My father stays at Columbia for more than twenty years, writes a number of books, walks miles each day, and develops a chronic cough. Mother volunteers at Riverside Church and takes care of her mother, who lives to be ninety-six. In 1982, Mother and Father make their final move, to the Bridgewater Retirement Village in Virginia. Father continues to walk miles each day, alone. My parents move into our home in Stanley in 2002. Father dies after several weeks; Mother remains with us until her death in 2007.

I e-mail and talk with Roger from time to time.

$\mathcal{F}$ E A R

Fear. I have only one fear. I remember it clearly from age ten on, but my mother reminded me that I had asked questions about it when I was four or five. I am afraid about nothing other than this one condition. All else is mere anxiety about aligning details and circumstances. And any happiness-over-nothing intrudes only briefly and intermittently over the all-encompassing doom, the terror—not fear—the terror of annihilation, cessation of being, disappearance, death. My mother reminds me that I asked, "Why does Jesus make us die?" at age four or five. I woke in the middle of fever nights screaming: a cement box and no way to call to my parents, whose figures I saw outlined in the doorway. I could not escape dreaded scenarios of the earth stopping turning, of floating off into space, of worlds crashing, the sun going out, of sudden nothingness.

Fear of death has produced every turning in my life, every leaving, every trip, every new acquaintance or encounter. Holding close in the nighttime, tears of comfort or calming, mistaken for passion and love, and never to last more than a year or two or three.

So happiness is floating, and joy is in the moment, when a touch of beauty intrudes and covers the background of fear. Out the window, the sun is shining, it's peaceful, green, wind blowing, and I thank God. I am happy to be writing, and it's an unexplainably happy morning.

PRETEND NOT TO CARE

Mother killed my bird. Bird was also his name, and he was a Java rice sparrow, and he flew freely around the house, danced in front of the toaster on the kitchen table, seeing his reflection; flew pieces of string and bits of paper to nests he built behind the books in the case; and attacked anyone's finger coming near him. He wasn't unfriendly, just wild. The neighbor across the street, Mr. Oelhoff, had a business in New York City's harbor area repairing oceangoing ships. A sea captain gave him the bird. It was from the Far East, maybe even Java. We got Bird, and I never knew why Mr. Oelhoff made the offer. Beautiful bird, rose-colored beak, white cheeks, black cap, and orange rings around his eyes. Sleek gray, fast flying, and always around.

Mother killed my bird. In two stages. First, she wondered if our Bird wasn't lonely, and she brought home a pet shop rice sparrow. Of course, her choice was the saddest one in the lot, and it was frightened and shabby. No one asked about male or female, whether they'd get along, if there were any territorial issues. In any case, they didn't get along; the new bird would not venture outside its own cage, and any attempt to put them together failed. Then Bird seemed to get fidgety and itchy, and Mother figured there were lice or bugs in the cages or on the birds, so she went and bought a spray and doused Bird with it. In a few days he was dead, gone to the bottom of the cage and never got up. The bottle read clearly to spray only cages and bedding, never directly on a bird, and she had doused him. Dead.

I didn't mourn. We buried Bird in the yard, and Mother needed the consoling words. We just let it go. I do not know if I just pretended not to care, or if somehow I really didn't, and he just flew away, out of our lives. Bird died on my birthday in 1956, more than fifty years ago today.

HEROES AND CAPES
NEW JERSEY, 1953

I believe in heroes. Not stars, who tap their hearts, kiss their fingers, and point skyward in thankful triumph, but heroes. Stars are born of success and acclaim, nourished by competition, while heroes embark on improbable missions, succeed or fail in hopeless situations, and are defined and known by the quality of their causes. Adoring crowds cheer the star, while the hero's beneficiaries are relieved and comforted, surprised and overwhelmed by unexpected gratitude, by mercy.

At ages eight and nine and ten, we played in the yard, around the house. We lived in a safe and small and comfortable neighborhood. We played Lone Ranger and desperadoes, Superman and super-villains, Zorro and hapless Mexican guards, or simply good guys and bad guys. Later, when we began to understand the world, we played Castro's ragtag and righteous band in pursuit of an evil Batista, or Americans in pursuit of the Russian sputnik. But the defining line in our minds and hearts and actions was clearly drawn, always, between right and wrong, between good and evil, between mercy and shame.

We did not have television in our house and sometimes stood silently in the neighbors' yard, watching TV through their window. But we listened to the radio and read Marvel comic books. We learned about truth and pure motives, about arriving just in time to save the day, and about the sadness of a hero's death. And we had capes. We had capes that captured the speed and urgency and rightness of our adventures. We were rich with capes, and I am sure, at the time, we flew.

My mother sewed the capes, and mine was regal purple, flowing, lined with rich golden yellow on the underside. I never knew if the matching golden script letter *S* in the middle of the purple back was for "Superman" or for "Scott," my more usual name. I never asked. My brother Roger's cape was brown and a dull reddish-orange, and I do not recall if he too had an *S* on the back, or more logically, an *R* for Roger. Neither do I recall if we wore the capes at all times, or just in play.

We grew up in a time and in a neighborhood that invited us to practice heroic roles, encouraged us to fly to right wrongs and relieve distress, and taught us to process children's circumstance with righteous filters. We found it no unusual or special wonder to wear a cape. A hero's cape.

S H A M E

Whether to buy it or not. The red tractor-trailer was on the upper shelf. It was a livestock carrier, a single-axle International day-cab tractor, but the trailer had bogey wheels, bright red, and a long cardboard carton to carry it home. I had the six dollars to buy it, and no particular need to keep the money, with a dollar-fifty allowance per week and plenty saved up. The question was the size of the truck and the utility, the question of need. My Dinky Toys were small and cost lots less—sixty-five cents or a dollar or two, at most. Easy to hide, and easy to allow; they didn't stand out or have luxury price tags. This was 1954 or 1955.

I could not decide. Carrying the large carton into the house would be difficult to cover, difficult to hide. Bus ride from the toy store in Englewood home to Leonia.

I bought the toy truck. Hid it under my bed, and never played with it in the open. Gave it away when we moved to Minnesota.

$\mathcal{T}$HE $\mathcal{B}$ICYCLE

We got bicycles for Christmas. We knew it and figured they'd be used, but at least we'd be able to ride with the neighborhood kids. Father said to stay out of the basement, and we could smell paint, so we wondered what color the bikes would be.

Christmas morning, the bikes stood at the tree in the living room, and I knew which was mine. Roger's was tall and responsible, rich fresh red with rear side baskets for his paper route, which, until now, he walked. Roger's bike was clean, straight, hardworking, and patient. Father had painted it.

Mine was not repainted. I remember not knowing what to think. It was bright yellow-orange, with wheels and tires painted silver. Silver tires. Paint on rubber. The fenders had chains of black diamonds stretched from front to back down the middle of the fender and black pinstripes to match. My bike was low-slung and indescribably foolish, fast, and sassy. It wasn't me, but it was mine. High Street, where we lived, dropped down from Broad Street, and I could lock the brakes coming down the hill and slide sideways to a stop, slide twenty feet in front of our house. We moved to Minnesota the next year and left the bike in New Jersey.

$\mathcal{W}$ I N D O W

Leonia, New Jersey, 1953 to 1958. 136 High Street, a block west of Broad Avenue. We lived in a comfortable older home, and we each had a bedroom for the first time. We owned the home, cost sixteen thousand, and it's probably worth a half million today. But my room was on the second floor, my bed against the front wall, at the same height as the windowsill—only six inches or so above the porch roof that extended across the entire front of the house and around the western corner. But I had a view of the night sky, the tall trees that lined the quiet street, and the rain. When it rained, the splatter of the raindrops came through the screen in the finest mist, cool and calm, fresh and full of the scent of night. Better even when it thundered; lightning, summer night storm, and the sounds of rain-clatter on the roof mingled with every other sense of this wonder.

My window-side joy and comfort as a fourth or fifth or sixth grader lived on, though I never had such an actual bedtime view on the world as I had in Leonia. I developed a dream about rain outside my window, and the dream joined with others, that it would be with beautiful, bohemian first lover-girl Stevie, that it would be my apartment, New York, in Greenwich Village, rain spattering on the fire escape, third floor up. Arms in the night, soft music, freedom, rain outside my window. Heaven.

WORDS AND LONELINESS

From my father I learned that words captured ideas, and that one could formulate a future working at one's desk with pen and paper. My father wrote at his desk in the study. He was chaplain at Carleton in our youngest years, and he read his sermons to us at the dinner table, turning off the classical music station before clearing his throat and reading. Fifteen or twenty minutes at the most, and my brother Roger and I didn't understand much of what he was saying, but the logic and the clarity were obvious. He was convincing, we were sure, ideas and encouragements and facts and beliefs crafted into a predictable shell.

What I learned was very different from what my brother learned. I sat and took it in, a five-year-old understanding the weight of words, and my brother, six years old, likely began to make ultimate plans for escape, for refusal, for rebellion. The tension in the dining room was as tight as the silence surrounding the speech. We sat, waited impatiently for the end of the exercise. Release came shortly, we were excused from the table, and Roger left to pursue his own interests while I ran to play, to ride, to draw, to find friends. But I am sure my soul heard the words, the construction, the flow of ideas and arguments, the logic, the surety, the possibility.

But the other thing I learned from my father was loneliness and isolation and rootlessness. He was restless, moving from job to job, from study to study, traveling extensively as if to find something, and ended in a quiet and lonely retirement. I am sure that my father was deeply afraid of death, and that he never rested comfortably. My father had many colleagues, but no real friends. I know that I never experienced him in any setting with other persons, in storytelling, light entertainment, tender sharing, enjoying food, having confidently quiet moments. Never. So, from my father, I have gained the surety of words and ideas, and the transience of existence.

Mother, Aunt Vivian, and Grandmother

I remember my mother, her sister Vivian, and their mother. My grandmother Gena Branscombe Tenney was a refined lady, a preeminent female composer, a Canadian and Royalist, and she viewed every accomplishment in the world as "marvelous." Things were wonderful, well done. Marvelous. And she added pepper to instant mashed potatoes, which my father would not eat.

Likewise my mother's sister, Aunt Vivian, or just Vivian, served roast beef, which, as a ten-year-old, I had never tasted before. Aunt Vivian was a physician, a surgeon, specialist in psychosomatic causes of diseases, and she traveled the world each year, to the most distant conference on her specialty, psychosomatic causes of cancer in humans. Vivian's roast beef was rich and delicious, as was her stroganoff and anything else she served in her East Side New York apartment. All the dishes were Stouffer's. Frozen, delicious, rare luxury.

My mother burned food, on the telephone instead of minding the liver and onions and bacon: weekly trials. Her meatloaf was garnished with ketchup, baked crusty—not bad, but careless nevertheless. Also a weekly showing, a regular cycle of low-key fare. At ten, having tasted roast beef at Aunt Vivian's and pepper in instant mashed potatoes at Grandmother's, I began to cook for myself.

39

An aside: I met Aunt Beatrice, my mother's and Vivian's surviving sister, only once, also when I was about ten years old. A fourth sister, Betty, had died in the flu epidemic of 1918, a couple years old. Aunt Beatrice was pale, thin, and worried. She sat at the evening dinner table and was quiet and polite. She struggled with unnamed battles, and we received the news calmly when she died. We never learned exactly how Beatrice died.

Aunt Vivian's marriage had been annulled, due to husband John's insistence that Vivian give up her medical practice, since she was married.

Grandmother Tenney's husband John died at age sixty, and she lived to be ninety-six, staying in her own New York City studio, Steinway grand piano in the one living-bedroom. I remember the Tenney women: Gena, my mother; Gena, my grandmother; and Vivian, Mother's sister.

$\mathcal{M}$ A S H E D $\mathcal{P}$ O T A T O E S

My mom made perfect mashed potatoes. She didn't know that she did, and didn't apply any pride or boasting to it, but she did. She boiled the potatoes and then ran them through a Foley food mill. Round and round, reversing to scrape the skins off the little holes in the base of the mill. Three or four swings around and then a grinding reverse. She'd bang out the peels that jammed up the holes rather than peel the potatoes before mashing them. I don't think it was for any laziness, but because if peeled, valuable potato would be lost to the garbage can. The potatoes were flavored by the small amounts of potato skin that made it through the mill, and with the milk and margarine and salt, we got mashed potatoes that tasted like whole, boiled potatoes. Good. The best.

I didn't learn about pepper or about instant mashed potatoes until we visited my grandmother's apartment in New York. Long, dark corridor, eight rooms on the first floor of a dark apartment building on 114th Street, West Side. Grandmother Tenney didn't cook much, and we were invited to eat only one time that I can remember. I was probably ten years old. She served mashed potatoes that my father would not touch, because they had pepper in them. I did not understand why he wouldn't eat them, but I guessed it was about the little black flecks, which I had never seen before. Pepper. He told me years later that he thought pepper was unhealthy. Grandmother Tenney's potatoes had a bright white color, which highlighted the pepper, and when I tasted them, I noticed the lightness, the saltiness, something so unlike my mother's rich and heavy fare. Pepper. Instant mashed potatoes. Salt. Light. Spicy. No bother, no fuss. No banging. No food mill. Good.

COOKING SCHOOL 1

I loved the breakfasts I cooked. I was ten, maybe eleven. Leonia, New Jersey. It was easier to cook my own than to eat what came our way. My father cooked scrambled eggs and oatmeal on alternate days. Without any disruption in the schedule. I asked him once if we could have the scrambled eggs two days in a row, because I liked eggs and didn't like oatmeal. He said no, and then we would have to have oatmeal two days running, anyway.

But I could cook my own. I asked my mother to buy bacon, and she did, because she didn't really mind—or care. I fried the bacon, scrambled eggs real soft, three or four, toasted English muffins, applied too much butter and served all on the Blue Willow plates. I got out my camera and took a picture of the plated food. I was satisfied, and from then on, I made my own breakfasts, ate what I wanted and as much as I pleased, and learned to clean up carefully to hide what I had made.

Three years later, in Northfield, Minnesota, I got the idea that I could make hamburgers and sandwiches for the students who lived in the dorm next door—Carleton students. My mother and father took this as a project and assisted in planning and the cost accounting. I made menus and a small ad to post in the dorm. At the last moment, my father nixed the idea, understanding that his position as dean of the college might make it an unwise project. For him.

I was going to serve hamburgers and sandwiches, and they would have been terrific.

$\mathcal{L}$EAVING $\mathcal{H}$OME—
$\mathcal{N}$ORTHFIELD, 1960

Northfield, Minnesota was my one chance, and my last chance, to have a hometown, to invest and connect deeply, heart and place and people. I was thirteen when my father told us he would be leaving the deanship at Carleton College after only two years and returning to New York, to the same faculty position at Teachers College he had left to bring us for a third sojourn in Northfield.

When I was a year or two old, we had lived on Northfield's First Street, and I remember only the hard, short, dusty grass in the small front yard, close to the hot summer sidewalk and street. Several years later, we moved back to Northfield from New Jersey and New York, to the first floor of a big stucco house on Second Street, for my kindergarten and first grade years. Five years later, we made our last move to Northfield from Connecticut and New Jersey and Wisconsin, back to that same house on Second Street, for seventh and eighth grades at the junior-senior high school only a block away on Third Street. Three attempted plantings, then uprootings, and we're leaving again.

But this was different. Not simply another move in the dozen or so since I was born in New York City. I was leaving a first teenage love, Brigid, and I was going to a boarding school in Pennsylvania. The options while living with my mother and father in the City, on the Upper

45

West Side, were either to attend a fancy day prep school in Manhattan or the thousands-student George Washington High School further up Amsterdam Avenue. Bleak choices, after Northfield. The prep and co-ed boarding schools were luxury options we could never afford, but they were part of Columbia's program to attract faculty with families to the Morningside Heights campus on the edge of Harlem.

To make matters worse, in Northfield, Brigid, my first real girlfriend ever, was also moving away. I had never put my arm around a girl in true tenderness before Brigid. The actual relationship, which consisted of long walks and several embraces, lasted no more than a month or two or three in the Minnesota spring before we left, though a lonely and wistful fallout persisted in my mind and heart for three or four years after we moved, maybe longer. Memories, and wondering: what if we had both stayed in Northfield? Even fifty years later, I had a faded photo of the Minnesota girl pinned to my principal's office bulletin board, partly to reassure lovelorn teens that life goes on, survives, improves. I point to the photo. "Son, my first true love. And do you know where she is today?"

"No, where?"

"I don't know. I got over it. I'm happily married. Lots of great girls waiting out there."

Our last year in Northfield, Brigid's dad died one night in his sleep, and her mom gathered the two daughters and their things and planned their move to California. East coast boarding school for me, California sunshine for Brigid, three thousand miles. Gloomy prospects at the time, for a fourteen-year-old hanging on to the thought of love.

Northfield was the only place I might have called my hometown. It was quiet and honest, surrounded by creeks and a beautiful river, by fields, and wind and snow. The springtime was true rebirth, ice jams breaking up on the Cannon River, wind blowing across Pine Hill, where we walked, and futures just beginning to be crafted and dreamed beyond childhood imagination. I drove a tractor, pulling the hay wagon, and had regular friends who lived within warm and tight-knit families invested in either the land or the town or the college—two colleges actually; Carleton and Saint Olaf. The highway sign on the outskirts of town promised "Cows, Colleges, Contentment." It was almost my hometown.

My father's plan to leave Carleton College was a usual scenario, one that we were beginning to recognize: his disappointment with the current place and plan, revitalized energy for the new, and once again it was to return to a place he had already been and abandoned. My mother was not in agreement and talked of staying on in Northfield with the boys, my brother and me. She was heartbroken about the prospect of us leaving home. My brother, a year older, would also attend boarding school, at another Quaker school in Pennsylvania: our parents' plan to keep us from competing with each other through the teen years. So, I was leaving home at a young age, leaving family, my brother, my one-time touch and imagination of a girlfriend, and what could have been hometown. Northfield.

The several years that followed contained growing-up activities often reserved for after high school, first jobs, showing classroom movies in Teachers College summer school courses, making taffy and washing pots and waiting table in Cape May, New Jersey, preparing for college. At boarding school, I had enough pocket money to buy clothing and entertain hobbies, played sports, and had a string of girlfriends. I traveled as well. My brother and I hitchhiked to Florida one school vacation from New York, making it only to Georgia before turning back; I drove with

Dave Hollister, a high school friend, to Northfield one winter break, just to visit for a day, finding only one or two junior high school friends in the neighborhood.

A couple of years later, another high school pal and I drove west and on the way back stopped in Northfield. I learned from my upstairs friend Jimmy Nelson, on Second Street in Northfield, that Brigid's mom had moved back to Minnesota and that Brigid was living in Stillwater, east of the Twin Cities, that she was working a summer job in a bank before she returned to college.

We drove the hour or so north to Stillwater and got to the bank after 3:00 p.m. The plate glass front door was locked, but I could see Brigid inside, behind a counter, and knocked. She looked puzzled and came to the door. She was different, older, more grown up. I had to explain who I was through the door, too loud, and she turned and got some permission, opened the door, and came out. We talked awkwardly for five or ten minutes, having nothing much in common to relate, and I said good-bye, thanked her for coming out to talk, that it was nice to see her. I do not recall anything she might have said.

I have returned to Northfield only once since, driving south from a conference in Minneapolis in a rented car. I drove past the two houses we lived in, through the Carleton campus, cruised the main streets, the Jesse James Days ads on display, parked on a dusty lane, and walked to the top of Pine Hill. I stayed overnight in the hotel on Main Street and drove back to the Twin Cities the next morning. I knew I was leaving Northfield for the last time and knew in my heart that I had already left home, my one-time hometown, my childhood, so many years before.

A Hill I Once Knew

I once knew Pine Hill. Pine Hill is just above Carleton College in Northfield, Minnesota. I knew Pine Hill in my junior high school years, seventh and eighth grades, 1958 and 1959. There was a single tree at the top of the hill, grassy slope, not too steep, an easy walk for a boy and girl. There was a single rounded stone, a rock, at the top, near to the tree. Pine Hill was a windy place, open sky and warm breeze in the summer, fresh wind in the springtime when the ice was breaking up on the Cannon River below. We sat on the rock and held hands. We lived in different worlds, as this was new to me, to walk slowly in a side-by-side embrace, no kiss, no hug, nothing that perhaps she had already experienced. Bill Kolb or Danny Spartz, who had a car and played guitar in a band. We had silence, and I had wish and wonder, all tied up with Pine Hill.

$\mathcal{E}$ D D I E

I got word that Eddie had died while I was at summer camp in northern Minnesota. It was a hot day, and we were playing ball. This was June or July after my ninth-grade year, so it would have been at least three years since I had seen Eddie. He lived in a house on the next street over in Leonia, New Jersey, and our backyards touched at one corner, bushes, fences, and crawl spaces marking the border. I didn't like Eddie, and we even fought once, but the news of his death hit me in the pit of my stomach: life and then death, a boy my age, suddenly. My mother sent a copy of the newspaper article someone had mailed to her from New Jersey. I remember how hot the sun was as I took the news in, walked around the softball field where we were playing ball, shocked at the news about the death of a boy just my age. I told a camp counselor about it, and he tried to comfort me, but I wasn't upset, just shocked. Surprised, at such news.

Eddie had been playing baseball, little league, batting, and the pitcher's throw hit Eddie and he swallowed his chewing gum and it gagged him and he died, not able to breathe, vomit filling his lungs. The ball hit him in the abdomen, the article said, the pit of his stomach, life and death, suddenly, unexpected, unnecessary. I had never heard the word "abdomen" before. The counselor told me it was his stomach, low.

I remember the last time I saw Eddie, in sixth grade. My friends told me that Eddie had said some really bad things about me and that he wanted to fight. I don't recall what it was about, but I thought he and his brothers were pretty mean, and I guess it was their way, or just my fear. I had never been in a fight, or even argued with anyone, but my friends said it would be best to take care of it right away. I walked across the backyard, brushed through the bushes, and went around to the front of his house, rang the bell. Eddie's younger brother came to the door, and I asked to speak to Eddie. He came to the door and looked at me, and before he could say anything, I punched him once, hard, in the stomach. Cowardly shot, low, probably the abdomen. I ran as fast as I could, heard Eddie yelling for his brothers, and their footsteps and shouts following behind me.

I ran as fast as I could, too afraid to fight, through the bushes and across the yard, around to the front and in our front door. Eddie and his brothers pounded up onto the porch, made a lot of noise, walked back and forth, shouting. After a while, they left. I did not go outside that afternoon. We moved to Minnesota soon after, and Eddie and I never did fight. I have often wondered if he was chewing gum that day.

$\mathcal{G}$LORY

It was fitting glory, in that my brother and my mother were present. The George School track team was at Westtown School, where my brother went, and my mother was at his parents' day. There was a track meet, and everyone was there. I normally ran the half mile and did high jumping, but they had a special four-mile relay, four legs of one mile each, and I was to run the first leg. My brother was at the track with our mother, her usual beaming with pride.

I think it was real pride, but I could not help remembering the only other time she came to a track meet: my first quarter-mile run in Northfield, seventh grade, maybe eighth. I didn't know how to run at the time and sprinted out to an immediate long lead, most particularly because Mother was there. I led most of the race, and then with perhaps a hundred yards to go, something began to happen to my legs and within several paces, I began to falter and slow and was passed by one, then another, and more, and finally all the other runners. Dead last, beaten and gasping for air, no legs under me. I was ashamed and without an excuse, but Mother beamed with pride, real I think. "Weren't you wonderful! I've never seen anyone run so fast, you were way in the lead! I couldn't believe it!" *And finished last,* I thought. "Let's celebrate," she offered, and we drove to Main Street and had supper together at the Collegiate Café, just her and me. I remember the chopped hamburger steak and mashed potatoes, and cottage cheese. Like it was yesterday.

So this day, five years later, and I had learned something about running and did well as a rule, but the mile wasn't my race, as I had gained some weight. I ran with the lesson learned in Northfield, pace and relax, just stride on out and breathe easy, in and out, music in my head. Four laps. I saw Roger and Mother at the side, and Roger was shouting me on. He didn't compete, at anything, actually, as far as I knew, and he was shouting excitedly, for me. Four laps, and halfway through the third lap, I passed the Westtown runner straggling along, maybe my Northfield self, then breezed through the fourth lap, our team with more than a quarter-mile cushion, and we won handily. It was a sweet victory, the second of two times my mother watched me run, and I remember so clearly the chopped hamburger steak at the Collegiate Café. That was really good.

$\mathcal{P}$ACK OF $\mathcal{K}$ENTS

I rode home for spring vacation in a car driven by a teenager from New Jersey, Elliot's or Mark's brother, I don't remember. Four eleventh-grade boys in a car, Pennsylvania to New York City. Anxious for free time, trading school and Bucks County trees and rolling hills for a week with family. They dropped me in the City and agreed to pick me up for the return trip, time and place set, we had bonded on the ride home. The driver had offered me and the others a smoke, and I heard my casual "Sure" echo Mark's and Elliot's. Two hours' small talk and silence, drawing in the smoke and breathing freedom and danger, a sad and lonely new song.

Suitcase on the pavement, I stood on the corner, 120th Street, Upper West Side, and waited to go through the doors, take the elevator to the sixth floor. The car pulled away from the curb, brief waves through the window.

A week. I had a week to be the casual smoker in the car. The drive and the miles and the careless bonding of men and cigarettes required it. The habit would come later, but this draw was even greater than nicotine. I knew that I needed my own cigarettes to offer, a pack. My parents did not smoke; nor did my older brother, but the practice wasn't forbidden or scorned, and I remember as a young child seeing my dad's cigarette case on the coffee table for visitors or faculty from the college, casual.

I didn't smoke during the week off, but planned on buying a pack before the return trip to school, easy enough. Saturday before the drive back, I walked across Amsterdam Avenue to Hartley's Chemists and bought a pack of cigarettes, to share, Kent, soft pack. Kent. In 1957 I gave my fifth grade teacher, Mr. Stanaland, a carton of Kent cigarettes for Christmas, because I really admired him and my mother said I could give him a present, my first male school teacher. Kent cigarettes, Micronite filter, gray-white pack. I remember the carton cost two dollars and ten cents. I don't know what one pack cost in 1963, but it felt priceless.

I waited on the corner for Elliot and Mark Sunday afternoon. I was not unhappy to return to school, but the future was beginning to take on new and uncertain shapes, of prolonged study aimed at careers, or work and war, and persistent dreams of wistful women and travel. But for the day, boys in a car, and I had a pack of cigarettes in my shirt pocket. Unopened, ready for a casual smoker in the car, part of the gang. On time. The car rattled down the cobblestone street, slowed, and made a wide U-turn. In a flash of realization, I opened the fresh pack of Kents, tore the foil top, and shook out four or five cigarettes into the gutter, crushed the pack lightly, and put it back in my pocket. Casual pack, casual smoker. In the car.

$\mathcal{L}$EARNING TO $\mathcal{D}$RIVE

Mom decided that the boys needed to be able to drive, in case an emergency arose. She decided this while we were on a camping vacation in northern Minnesota, on the Gunflint Trail, in the woods. We were in seventh and eighth grades, so it wasn't an outlandish idea. We each got a chance to try, but Roger turned it down, just didn't want to, and I stalled the car—stick shift, of course—three or four times, and we all gave up.

Four years later, in Pennsylvania, sixteen years old, eleventh grader, I learned to drive. Out of the blue the opportunity came to sign up for driver's education. The driver's ed teacher was the father of one of my classmates at George School, a heavyset man who drove an old Nash Rambler. The car had no special dual controls or brakes for the instructor. He sat back and told me to start up the car. "Put it in neutral and push in the clutch anyway, and turn the ignition. Give it a little gas."

Everything worked fine, the car started, he told me how to let out on the clutch slowly and where the brakes were, in case we had to stop. He laughed when he told me that. In case we had to stop. Within minutes we had left school and were rolling smoothly down the highway toward Langhorne, where my girlfriend lived. She has no part in this story.

As I remember now, it was evening, almost dark. Learning to drive. We motored along uneventfully until we came to the steep hill that runs up to Langhorne, under the Pennsylvania Railroad tracks, a cement and brick underpass. The hill was steep, and the car slowed some. And at this point, I received the only real instruction in driving I have ever gotten.

"Give it the gas, boy, let's go up this hill. Floor it!"

We flew, and I never looked back. Freedom.

COLLEGES

I drove to Texas once, in 1963, to visit Southern Methodist University. SMU. I have no recollection of why I included SMU on the short list of colleges I would apply to: Boston College, UNC, Antioch, and SMU. What was I thinking? A Jesuit college, the all-male campus at North Carolina, my brother's choice, in Ohio, and a sandstone football college in the blazing Texas sun. But the four were strategically placed for a trip around the country in my hundred-fifty dollar 1949 Buick convertible, to visit my college choices, to help decide which one. Of course, any one would have been the same disaster UNC turned out to be; I packed my burdens and baggage and took them wherever I went.

UNC was the prettiest place, while SMU was bright and treeless, hot and glaring. I spent a moment or two on each campus, walked here and there, looked back and forth, and drove on. I loved driving, top down, radio blaring, freedom, and the few dollars I had saved, my father underwriting the gas, allowing the journey because of the school visits. It was all just enough, barely worth the effort, but I was free. South from New Jersey, where I garaged the car.

A day to UNC, one or two more to Dallas and SMU, stopping in New Orleans for something to eat only, as the entire city smelled bad. On to Shreveport and Dallas, north through the Oklahoma panhandle, across

61

the corner of New Mexico, Raton, in the mountains, through Denver, and on to Cheyenne, Wyoming.

The car broke down six miles outside Chugwater, Wyoming, as I carelessly shifted the car into low gear while speeding down a long hill, speeding top down in a rain shower, turn signal and automatic gearshift on the same side of the steering column. Towed to Cheyenne to get the car fixed. The transmission job would eat up most of the money I had, and I was sidetracked in a cheap motel for several days while they fixed the car. The garage offered to trade my car for a cheaper ride, a Rambler, but I loved the car and my trip. The transmission cost one hundred forty-nine dollars to fix, a dollar less than I had paid for the car, and I had just enough money. Just.

My father was at a conference—"Week of Work," they called it, a summer gathering for college professors, this year in South Bend, at Notre Dame. Our family used to attend the conference, and it was a special joy, quiet and reserved, lots of kids. I called my father, told him I was stuck, and then headed his way, scraping the last dollars together for gas and a straight shot across the plains and the Midwest.

My college visits, two so far, UNC and SMU, had taken no more than ten days altogether, including the repair, and I relaxed at Notre Dame, driving other professors' kids around in my old black Buick, top down, radio blaring. I had no clue where I was headed, despite plans to visit brother Roger in Ohio, at Antioch, to drive him and some of his friends back east. No clue.

MUSIC

I play the piano. I learned about music early, as my mother was a professor of music and a conductor; her mother was a composer of note, and my father's mom had played viola in a Midwestern orchestra. We listened to WOR radio at the dinner table, and my mother and father guessed at the names of composers based on the style and nature of the piece being played. Their game. I learned about notes and scales, playing the violin in the elementary school orchestra, drums, and then piano. My father tried to learn to play his mother's viola, but he could not match skill with his notion of beautiful music.

Larry Cremin was my dad's boss and department chair at Columbia. He went on to be president of Teachers College, but in 1956 or 1957 he came to visit in our home and played the piano for us. He played boogie woogie and showed one or two of the elementary bass patterns and the basic right-hand chords. Key of C. Turned out he had written a music book for beginning boogie woogie piano playing, which he sent to the house. I practiced, learned walking bass and several of the basic pieces, and played all the time. My mother arranged fresh music lessons, and I learned a little more, but did not practice anything other than boogie woogie. It's all I know to play, though I've learned to play one or two complex jazz numbers from memory. Mostly forgotten, except the boogie woogie. Mostly key of C, some in F.

I fancy an understanding of basic bass lines in the most fundamental rock and pop music and love it all. Classical, mom and dad set the stage; rolling bass, thank you Larry Cremin. Pop music, always part of the melancholy time stamps, I can supply the counterpoint and harmony.

GREENWICH VILLAGE PIANO

It was a bar in Greenwich Village. When we visited the city, my high school friends and I stayed at my parents' house, and as soon as possible we headed south, on the subway, for Christopher Street and the Village. The drinking age was eighteen, so the later trips we took included beer and wine, if at least one of us had turned eighteen. We were in a bar in the village and had drunk a lot of beer. So we were smooth and wise and had the run of the place, only a few other patrons this evening.

"Scottie, play the piano," from one of my friends. And I did, boogie and a little jazz, and it was excellent, flowing and in tune, some shouting and clapping, and my friends reminded me of the enjoyment many times in the years to come. But they didn't know the truth.

I visited the bar the next year, maybe two. I drank a few beers and longed to play the old piano in the corner. I was alone and had no cheerleaders. After an hour of wondering and waiting, and drinking beer, I asked the bartender if I could play the piano.

He said "Sure, why not?" And I did. The keys did not work well, and the piano was out of tune. I struggled through a single boogie number, glad I had the nerve to finish it. I returned to the bar stool and drank a last beer and left.

₵OOKING ₷CHOOL 2

I remember. I graduated from high school in 1964. George School, a top-flight, Quaker boarding school in Bucks County, Pennsylvania. Nearly all the grads went on to college. My friend Tom Parry and I talked about going to the Culinary Institute of America in Poughkeepsie, New York, learn to cook, open restaurants, whatever. I told my plans to my father, and he did not respond, really, not one way or the other. In fact, I do not remember what he said exactly; actually, I do remember. He said nothing.

The idea died a quiet death, and I applied to Boston College, UNC Chapel Hill, Antioch College, and SMU. I was accepted at all four, and I visited UNC, Antioch, and SMU during the summer of 1963, eventually choosing UNC. I remember that SMU was very hot and dry, baking in Dallas sun. Antioch was comfortable, and my brother Roger attended there. I visited him in my old Buick and stayed there several days while he finished exams, waiting to drive him and some friends home to New York. While I waited, I worked on a farm, having driven out to the countryside and offered my services. I drove the big John Deere A-model tractor with hay wagon hitched. I felt like a man of work and all abilities.

I chose UNC at Chapel Hill and entered in the fall of 1964. I was lost in a sea of Southern gentlemen, V-neck sweaters monogrammed over the heart, tassel loafers, genteel, polite, and mean, given the times. And

I did not know that Chapel Hill was all guys. A roommate asked if I was going to the dance.

"Dance? Sure. Where is it?"

"In the parking lot."

"Parking lot?"

"Yah, that's where the buses come in."

"Buses?"

"Yah, the girls, from Greensboro."

"Greensboro? "

"Yah. The women's college."

"Oh." I left Chapel Hill in March.

$\mathscr{A}$ $\mathscr{M}$ OVEABLE $\mathscr{F}$ EAST

This is a great book, Hemingway's remarkable memoir. Stevie gave me a copy, no, wrote me after I left North Carolina in 1965, told me of her love for the book. I've never read it through, I don't think, though I've bought copies several times and read pieces of it. I met Stevie in the month before I left UNC. I was lost, and she was beautiful, three years older, and graduating that spring. She was small and beautiful, really a tiny Joan Baez to look at, and one of the few women on campus. She planned our only date together, my last night in Chapel Hill, and was the first woman I slept with. She was pitiful and beautiful, wearing my T-shirt, on top of me in the dawning light, a friend's apartment in town, mattress on the living room floor. I left town on my Lambretta scooter later that morning.

Hemingway wrote *A Moveable Feast* in Cuba, in 1960 or so. He wrote about his time in Paris in the early 1920s. In the Cuban book he tells of writing pieces in Paris about Michigan winters. Thrice removed.

I ran into Stevie again only once, in the summer after I left Chapel Hill. Dave Erskine, my high school roommate, and I were walking in Greenwich Village, and she was in a café, drinking coffee at a table with a man I did not know. Improbable coincidence, to meet my first lover, North Carolina, in New York City on a summer night. We said hello, then went on our way. Of course, I had told Dave about her already, and he laughed and laughed, amazed at the coincidence, and I could tell he was pleased and relieved for me.

A LIE, OR TWO, AND MORE

I wasn't afraid, and I knew what I was doing. I had dropped out of college in the spring of 1965, surprised by UNC's attendance policy and the food in the cafeteria, and had no money. I got a job at US Steel in New York, mail room and then night shift computer center, running punch cards through the sorters. I knew that I would probably get drafted but had every intention of returning to college in the fall, and knew that the draft would understand this situation. When I talked with old high school friends, they appreciated my bold approach to things and praised my courage and planning.

When I received my draft notice, I hurried an application to Muhlenberg College, where Dave's dad taught, and was accepted. I took the acceptance letter to the draft physical, and they told me to strip and get in line. I went through the physical exam, not sure now that I'd be enrolling at Muhlenberg in September. What a coincidence when I failed the physical and received a ninety-day temporary deferment on the draft. I was sure this was a mere coincidence, and that once in college, I would have a student deferment.

I took the summer off, spent weeks basking in the Delaware River resort at Shawnee, Pennsylvania. Dave's father's Shawnee Island cabin on the river. I was ready for college in the fall and had all my plans in place.

$\mathcal{D}$ I D N ' T $\mathcal{F}$ I T

John and I applied for the Colgate job and got interviews. Route man, check stocks, visit ma-and-pa stores and supermarkets during the summer months. We were fraternity brothers, and he was a three-hundred-fifty-pound, confident football player, loud and seemed awfully mean. I was awkward and bright, cocky even, but lacked the surety needed to gain the confidence of the two business recruiters at Muhlenberg College that day. I stuttered and wondered at their questions. They smiled and nodded and thanked me after a brief exchange.

John got an offer, but turned down the job; I thought he must have felt it was beneath him, Colgate summer job. I drove a green 1950 Plymouth. As I recall, John's car was a big Chrysler, nice. When I came into the fraternity house, John sat in the living room.

"How'd it go?"

I don't remember what I said, but I found that he'd been offered a job on the spot, and I don't believe I knew what to say. I avoided those job interviews in the future.

PHONE CALL FROM JACK
EAST ORANGE, NEW
JERSEY, 1970

Holly answers the phone. It's very late, and I'm worn out. I'd rather not take the call. The day has been too long and a drain on my nerves. Holly had torpedoed the day early—the night before, actually. It was supposed to have been a fun Saturday with Pete and a few others who worked on the Dodd campaign, but Holly didn't want me to take part.

In the early fall, Pete Loos, a gym teacher at the Intermediate School where we teach, asks me to write releases and newspaper ads for Pat Dodd's bid for a seat in the New Jersey legislature. Lots of meetings, late-night sessions, northern Jersey wheeling and dealing. I'm not from East Orange, and it's fun to be included. Irish and Italian and Polish guys who joke and talk loud, eat with great enjoyment, play cards, and drink beer. Pat Dodd loses the race, but at the campaign thank-you dinner for workers and wives and husbands, Pete volunteers a great day, inviting some of the men to go out on his boat at Long Branch in the morning. He is putting the boat up for the winter and thinks it'll be fun to take a quick trip out on the ocean. Absolutely. Sure, great. Holly smiles her tight look reserved for *No* and says, "Sounds like fun."

"OK, I'm in," I answer. The battle begins on the way home.

"You're not really going, are you? With those guys?"

For once I stand my ground. I say that I am going, that we worked hard together for months on the campaign, and that I just want to go. "It'll be fun." The rest of the night is tense. Holly cries and gets sick, complaining that I can't leave her alone, sick. I say I am going to go, and do, early the next morning. It's a bitter exit, and a shamed and guilty day. Holly is sick often, but history says she will be fine if I stay home, so I go. I call a couple of times during the day, and she is OK. When I get home, she has baked a cake, and I guess that she has shamed her way through the day as well. Something new.

Holly has the phone. She says it's from Jack MacConnell. "It's Dr. MacConnell." Jack. Jack MacConnell, my education professor at Muhlenberg College. I am teaching language arts to fifth and sixth graders at the Intermediate School, thanks to Jack MacConnell. He was the enjoyable part of an unexciting student experience at Muhlenberg. He raced cars—hill climbs—had a big motorcycle, built a cabin, and hunted in the woods. Jack claimed Native American Indian blood and is blind in one eye. I minored in education simply because Jack MacConnell encouraged me. I also knew that a teaching job carried a likely deferment from the draft and the war. Vietnam.

I entered teaching with a passion, but find that it is a difficult battle day to day, and my actual teaching expertise is not impressive. I applied for jobs in New York City, but did not have the license, rode out to Newark, and was advised that East Orange needed teachers, even in English. At East Orange's Intermediate School, I am not a smooth or well-prepared teacher; rather, I gravitate toward extra duties supervising the lunch room and playground and am looking for a less troublesome teaching job in Bloomfield, tough and respect-filled Italian working-class town, neighboring the difficult and mostly black schools in East Orange and Newark.

Jack MacConnell is my second father of sorts, driving his sports cars and four-wheel-drive trucks and tramping through Pennsylvania's northern mountains and woods. His wife is easygoing and warm, and their home has been open to me, and to Holly as well, when we were students on campus. I do not know why he is calling so late on a Saturday evening.

"Hello, Dr. MacConnell."

"Jack. Sorry to call so late. I've got a question for you, and I hope you'll say yes, but you will need to do some things to get ready. Would you want to come back to Muhlenberg, teach in the department?" I do not understand. I am applying for jobs in Bloomfield and wonder if that's what he is talking about.

"What?"

"Bill French is retiring in two years. The dean says I am in line for head of the department. In two years. I'd like you to come and work with me in the Education Department. We could really make things more exciting around here." I think of Bill French and the only other professor in the department, old-timey Adeline Kreinheder, whom I knew well and who had studied with my dad at Columbia, where I was halfway through my master's degree.

"How about Dr. Kreinheder?" She was friendly, but I could already imagine an education department infused as much with race cars, motorcycles, and hunting trips as with children's literature and the history of education.

"She's retiring as well, the year after. It would be good to try some new things in the department. Two years from now—give it a thought. But you'll have to be working on your doctorate, at least be accepted in a program by then. Think about it. Two years."

"OK. I'll come see you. We could talk about it. Thanks, Dr. MacConnell."

"Jack."

"What did he want?" Holly asks. I explain it to her and wonder what it all means, how I could manage the studies. I thought of the job in Bloomfield. Two years, though. Holly and I talk.

Holly says, "You're not going to do it, are you?"

TURNER STREET
ALLENTOWN, 1973

It was clear when I got back to the apartment on Turner Street that she already knew. I was still in shock, having been at the lawyer's office, but she knew. I could see it on her face. It also reminded me of my thoughts from a week before, about the phone call she had taken. I had been surprised to see her at the apartment that day, and she had relayed a message about a phone call. "Somebody called. I don't know who it was. They didn't say what it was about." I could see. Her look had not matched her words. I had not had any particular reason to suspect anything but wished now that I had asked. I'm sure she would have told me. In any case, today I knew for sure, and it really didn't matter. Everything had changed.

We sat quietly on the sofa, not close. She was my friend and lover, signed on as the comfort in my mess of a marriage with Holly, the breakup, separation, and all the legal wrangling that followed. She was a welcome comfort, a bright spot in each day for almost a year, and didn't have any immediate demands. Holly would not hear anything about a divorce, would not even answer my calls or letters, and had a lawyer. Our two lawyers had a great thing going, Philadelphia to Allentown. But now everything had changed.

"I was at the lawyer's office," I said. I didn't ask if she somehow had known, but it was clear. She looked up and then away. "Holly's gone. The lawyer gave me a note from her minister. She died. Last week." Silence. "A note from her minister."

We sat quietly on the sofa, in front of the large, plate glass window. Turner Street traffic was heavy, two lanes, one-way downtown. It was a sunny Saturday in May; the school year was over. I looked out the window. Turner Street. Sounds of traffic. The divorce business was over. The waiting and the questions and the support payments and lawyer's bills were over. Everything had changed.

"The note said that Holly had been taken to be with the Lord. Thursday a week ago. Ten days. *Taken to be with the Lord.* The lawyer had a bill for me, too. One hundred forty dollars. When I called last week, he said everything was caught up, I didn't owe him anything. That's why he needed me to come to the office, to deliver the note from Holly's minister. One hundred forty dollars."

Quietly, "I'm so sorry." She knew that her position had shifted. A distance had already set in. She knew that her bright cheerfulness fit the past year's role, but less so, now. Distance. And once begun, the distance would increase, unstoppable. It was over. Like Holly's life. Death. I think I knew the same, though the reality would take time, a month or two, to set in, along with the relief from worry and uncertainty about a divorce.

Holly and I had been married for four years. We had been college sweethearts at Muhlenberg, in Allentown, where I now taught. She was a year younger than me. When I graduated and got my first job teaching, we drifted apart, but at a high school friend's wedding on a beautiful September day in Connecticut, we laughed and danced and then fought bitterly about jealousy, then made up. A few weeks later, we married. We ran off to Delaware for a weekend. My brother Roger and Dave, my best friend from high school and college, went along. We kept the affair quiet, as the college did not allow married students to remain on campus, and our marriage did not include any commitment to rush into a life together. Looking back, it was a foolish move that solidified nothing other than our lack of commitment and the deception. We never told our parents and married publicly in a big wedding orchestrated by Holly's mom the following June.

We did not know what surprises and turns and endings the coming years would hold. After Holly graduated and we married again, she joined me in East Orange. We both taught school there. Holly suffered with asthma and then added multiple sclerosis. I was invited to return to Muhlenberg College to teach in the Education Department, and Holly balked at that move, even though it brought her closer to her family home, outside Philadelphia. We seemed to very suddenly split apart.

We sat quietly. "I'm so sorry," she said again.

I wasn't sure.

Doctor's Appointment 1

I sat in the waiting room for the doctor's follow-up on my X-rays and tests. I had been light-headed for months, dizzy almost, and there was a question about my inner ear, something about the ear canal. I didn't know, but I hoped the doctor would make it clear. The nurse handed me my file to take in to the doctor, and then asked me to wait a bit. I sat and after a while began to page through the file, my file. It had blood tests, which I could understand only slightly, X-ray reports, and the radiologist's summary of what he saw. I scanned down the brief statement and stopped on the words, "suggests the possibility of a tumor." Tumor, cancer, and death, possibility and worry, death. I sat, stunned. This was it. I felt dizzy and light-headed, worse than usual. Everything else receded behind the curtain of my death's notice. The possibility of a tumor.

The nurse came to the door and showed me the way to the doctor's office. I handed him my file, sat, and he opened it. "Well, it looks like we'll do some more tests and X-rays, maybe in several months, to see how things change."

"What about the tumor?"

"Tumor? Who told you about any tumor?" He looked suddenly upset. With me.

"The file. In the file it says something about the possibility of a tumor."

"Who gave you the file? Why were you reading the file?"

"They gave it to me. It's my file, isn't it?" The doctor got up and went out. I heard him speaking to someone in the office. I do not remember anything more about the visit, but I did not return to the office.

DOCTOR'S APPOINTMENT 2

I sat in the waiting room for a new doctor's review of my X-rays and tests. I had been light-headed and dizzy for months, and there had been a question about my inner ear, the ear canal. I still didn't know, but I hoped this doctor would make it clear. I had been to another doctor, and he had been upset that I had read my file and found the mention in the reports of a possible tumor. My own angry reaction to that doctor had settled some of my light-headed feelings, and I put off doing anything about my problem for several months, worrying all the time about the tumor. But my girlfriend, an operating room nurse, suggested I see another doctor, one she knew was kind.

My new doctor had gotten the tests and X-ray reports from the first doctor, and I was to meet with him, find out what was going on. He greeted me in the waiting room and asked me to come in. He had the file in his hand.

"I understand you are concerned about your dizziness, and you have some pain with this?"

"No real pain, but I keep rubbing the back of my ear, and it feels funny."

"Well, not much to worry about. These kinds of things are not so uncommon, but it's not about anything really critical."

"The report said something about a tumor."

"Yes, well, that's not because the X-ray showed a tumor, just that the width of the ear canal on one ear is slightly wider than the other side, and there's always a question as to why that is so. Most likely, just because the one canal is a little wider than the other."

"Oh."

"So we should take X-rays in six months, maybe a year, see if there is any change in the difference between the two ear canals."

"Six months." I remember wondering how long I would have to worry about this.

"OK." Six months then.

"Yes. But I have talked enough. What questions do you have of me?"

$\mathscr{D}$OCTOR'S $\mathscr{A}$PPOINTMENT 3

I sat in the hospital waiting room, waiting for the radiologist to tell me the X-rays had turned out OK, and then I could go. He would send them and a report to my new doctor. I was in for the repeat X-rays on my ear canals, to see if there was any change in their respective widths. The variance between the two had raised the question in the original reports: the "suggestion of a tumor." That had scared me, but the doctor was more worried that I had seen the report, and he would not discuss it with me. Which scared me even more. My new doctor had simply said it was not serious, but to check it in six months, or a year, see if there was any change. So I stayed scared for another half year.

My light-headedness had persisted, and I rubbed behind my right ear all the time, wondering if the growing discomfort was the growing tumor somewhere beneath the surface. My best friend at the college kidded me about rubbing behind my right ear all the time. "Quit rubbing your head! It's nothing!" It was a consistent worry, and a constant sense of something behind my right ear. Death. The question of death. The radiologist bustled into the room.

"Do you have any pain at all, near your ear?" I was shocked, my worst fears confirmed. The radiologist looked really worried. I am dying.

"Pain? A little, I guess, yes."

"Where? Behind your ear?" More shock, sinking. I am dying.

"Show me where. If you would." He is young, pudgy, and sweating, worried.

"Right here." I reach up and slide my finger along the hairline behind my right ear.

"No, your left ear, the other side…"

$\mathcal{B}$ A R $\mathcal{F}$ O O D

Kern's was three blocks from the college. It was a bar and a restaurant, so we went there even before we could drink. They had burgers and steamed clams and Friday dinner specials, so people didn't treat the place like a bar—more like a family restaurant. Skip Kern ran the place, a big, football player type, and I remember his parents were still around, but he ran it. When I returned to Allentown to teach at the college, we went to Kern's for food or to drink beer with colleagues, some students even. Kern's did not contain any threat of drunkenness or impropriety; it was just warm and friendly and an easy place to go. I ate my first steamed clam at Kern's, an excuse to drink butter, I think. It was fatness and richness and luxury. Something my father or mother would never even imagine trying. My father particularly would never approach another person or place in random enjoyment, a casual encounter.

This reminds me of visiting a bar with my father in Ronda, Spain. He was on a personal study trip across Spain to trace the philosophy of Unamuno, the discredited social philosopher vilified by Franco. The university at Ronda, founded by Unamuno, had been destroyed by Franco, and my father and I were there; he invited me to join him after Holly died. We were in a bar, and he wanted so badly to know more about the university, about the philosopher's grand name, about the special richness of the place for him. But he could not ask. He held a glass of lemonade, and I had a beer. "Ask the bartender, Father. He'll know something." I spoke no Spanish, and my father was fluent, but he would not speak.

$\mathcal{P}$ IERRE AU
$\mathcal{T}$ UNNEL — $\mathcal{R}$ ECIPE

I could never duplicate the main-course dish from Pierre au Tunnel in New York. I ate there only once and guess it was one of their classical French offerings, simple and elegant, scampi provençal—maybe just shrimp scampi, though they wouldn't have used such a popularized description.

I do not know their trick or particular finesse, but it's simply a sauté of chopped garlic in clarified butter, perhaps green onions or shallots too, larger shrimp, a minute or two, add dry white wine, garlic, and freshly squeezed lemon juice, a pinch of salt and pepper, and fresh parsley. Maybe finish the sauce with a couple knots of cold butter. Serve on rice, I don't remember, but I've tried to match the experience many times and have never come close.

Pierre au Tunnel was my first experience with the finest everyday classical French cuisine. I did not know where I was, lunch on a slow-paced day in the City. Unexpected. Rich. A new world.

$\mathcal{L}$UNCH — $\mathcal{P}$AUL $\mathcal{B}$OCUSE

I booked lunch at Paul Bocuse three or four weeks in advance. We would drive to Lyon from Geneva and eat at the world's finest restaurant. Dinner reservations were nearly impossible and would cost too much anyway. This was an adventure I had only dreamed of, but I was working in Geneva, had a car to rent, a companion from the States, a small apartment, and time. I spoke enough French to get by, was scheduled to attend the *Hotelfachschule Luzern*, the Hotel Trades School in Luzern, had worked on and off, full- and part-time in kitchens for several years, and was excited to visit Bocuse.

The restaurant was not crowded; it seemed there were as many waiters and service personnel as guests. We ordered from the menu. Some of the dishes he was so well known for were there, including the bass in puff pastry, and I ordered an interestingly plain item with smoked salmon—cold, a nice starter. We had wine, and the service was impeccable. My salmon came, and it was a beautiful arrangement. And strangely enough, it looked like an excellent and elegant variation on a New York deli's nova lox, except Bocuse didn't include the onions. Ignorance and serendipity prevailed, and I asked the waiter if it was possible to have a little raw onion, chopped or sliced would be fine. He didn't understand my French, I guessed, so the maître d' joined the waiter and I asked again: a little raw onion, chopped; a little embarrassed this time. Eyebrows went up, and he said, "But of course," and they disappeared.

Within moments the waiter, maître d', and a cook in whites appeared, small bowl of chopped onion, all smiles, and they waited while I applied it to the plate. "Thank you" was not enough to clear them away, as they watched me eat a few bites and then retreated.

The meal was everything I had guessed it would be, excellent, crisp, fresh, an adventure. Until Paul Bocuse himself came out to greet the guests. He was shorter than I imagined, but cordial and graceful as he swished among the tables, smiling and making small talk. Clasped hands in front of his whites. He stopped at our table, and we exchanged only brief comments, as his English and my French were equally disturbing and we both insisted on being gracious, each using the other's language. I mentioned that I was going to take a course at Hotelfachschule Luzern. Swiss, German.

"Aha. You are a chef."

"No, not really; I have cooked some. Maybe someday."

"Perhaps you would like to see my other restaurant. In the country? I have a collection of mechanical circus steam organs, and one of the largest of such in the world. If you have time." This was nearly impossible to understand everything he said, in his English, but the invitation to join him was clear, and as unexpected as it was implausible. Paul Bocuse. Impossible.

"Yes, fine. Yes…" Chopped onion in a small glass bowl. An impertinent request.

GRAVAD LAKS—RECIPE

One frozen cold-water salmon, whole, partially thawed

    Trim tail, fins, and head to gills
    Cut into halves lengthwise along backbone
    Trim rib cage bones with flexible filet knife
    Pluck row of side rib bones with stainless steel pliers
    Leave skin on for handling and slicing.

    Rub flesh with equal parts sugar and salt, seasoned with white pepper
    Sprinkle generously with dried dill.

    Place two halves of fish flesh to flesh, tail to head
    Refrigerate, covered, twenty-four hours, turning once.
    Slice on bias to skin only (discard skin).

    Serve with rye bread and sweet brown-sugar mustard with dill.

    (May refreeze gravad laks after curing. For ease, slice when partially thawed.)

GENESEE BEER, GENEVA, 1976

My office is on the third floor of the International Labor Office in Geneva. The Bureau International du Travail. The BIT. Swiss. But maybe more French than Swiss. I have been here for nearly four months and have finished most of the work on a dull, hypothetical study in educational projects for profit in public schools. The idea for my research had taken shape about the same time my plane had landed in Geneva. My travel and project were the result of a special study grant intended to revitalize tired tenured faculty at Muhlenberg College, where I have taught for four years, Allentown, Pennsylvania. I am neither tired nor tenured, but I have not pictured my future there in Allentown clearly, or with any great sense of purpose.

In any case, I am finding that after two earlier trips overseas, I am increasingly drawn to the romance of travel and things European, particularly food and cooking. The older faculty at Muhlenberg College hadn't cared to take off a year at half pay, or even a half year at full pay, and only the less connected younger faculty applied for the three grants. I landed one. I've signed on for a six-month stint in Geneva and after that will attend the Swiss Hotelfachschule in Luzern, a professional culinary arts school, just for fun—and because my German is better than the French

97

I learned for this trip. I have taken off the entire year, leaving some time for what might happen.

After lunch this day, I page through the newspaper, the *International Herald Tribune*, and my mind's eye registers a special message, a small ad tucked away deep in the paper: "Genesee Beer Lovers, Where Are You?" I am in Geneva, Switzerland, first wondering and guessing, then knowing, remembering, why Genesee has placed the ad in an internationally distributed English-language newspaper. It's those television beer commercials, Genesee Beer. The TV ads so common back home in Pennsylvania. Ads built around a simple problem: Americans find themselves in far-off places that have special attractions, but no Genesee beer. Ads about Americans traveling in an exciting world, but missing their favorite beer. I have a cabin I built in Potter County, near Genesee, in northwestern Pennsylvania, and while I've never tasted the beer, I know the countryside is beautiful. I believe that I qualify as a truly possible lover of Genesee beer and feel justified in answering this ad. So I write to Genesee. Done, and put aside. No special thought, and in the casual pattern of days and events and life's remarkable unfolding, no idea how a cascade of coincidences beginning at Muhlenberg College in Allentown, Pennsylvania, will determine a decade's entanglement with Europe.

I put aside any thoughts of Genesee beer commercials. I have enough to worry about. I have two more months to work at the BIT, and the *Schools for Profit* piece I've nearly finished writing isn't very convincing. Another hitch—my friend Mary Ann from Allentown is coming to stay for a month or more, and I'm not confident about that. It will change the nature of my foreign adventure, for sure. But the view from my office window is still wonderful, and in a while I'll take a bus into the town and walk the back streets, look into the food shops, buy something interesting for supper. And maybe a bottle of wine, as I have no favorite beer in Switzerland.

But a month or so later, I hear from an ad agent in London. Barbara. She will be in Geneva and will interview me if I am available. We meet the following week. The interview is positive and enjoyable. Barbara is forgiving, letting me know that Genesee beer is brewed in Rochester, New York, not Pennsylvania. She accepts my description of Genesee beer, my favorite, as cold and crisp. Clear, mountain spring water. To me, still more Pennsylvania than Rochester, New York. Barbara thinks there might be some interest in combining my Swiss hotel trades school setting in Luzern with a Genesee commercial and says she will be in touch if things work out.

I do not hear from Barbara and close out my writing project. Likewise, Mary Ann and I part ways in Geneva, though she stays there, having fallen in love with the city and countryside. I make my trip to Luzern, find a room to rent, and prepare for the cooking school experience—which is not really in a school, but in the basement kitchen of the old and majestic Hotel Montana. Lake Luzern is dark, the old town is Middle Ages, all surrounded by steep mountains. Spectacular and romantic and mysterious. I am deeply moved by the air, the language, the mountains, the steam boats on the lake, the trams to the mountaintops, the wine, the food.

At the cooking school I am dubbed "*Mann aus Amerika*," the guy from America, and copy verbatim the chef instructor's recitations of ingredients and processes and cost calculations in tight, precise German into my notebook. Then we go to the kitchen and produce the dictated menu of the day, serve the students in the management and table service courses. Many, perhaps most, of the students are sons and daughters of Swiss hotel owners earning their certificates to take leading parts in the family businesses. While the romance of Luzern remains intoxicating, the cooking course is heavy-handed and dull, however textbook perfect. German.

Barbara phones me at the school. I get the call on a line in the kitchen's office. She has a proposal based on new ad agency travel plans and offers me one of the Genesee beer commercial spots. This involves flying to Spain, meeting the film crew and ad folks there, and doing a thirty-second commercial involving flamenco dancing, the Alhambra, and missing my favorite Genesee beer. They have rented a flamenco restaurant and dancer, a man and his burro, and a London model, to stroll with me in the Alhambra. Two or three days in Spain; in several weeks, Granada. Spain. Unfortunately, the timing is not possible, as I would miss the final week of my cooking course. No certificate.

At this moment, the chef instructor shouts from the walk-in cooler, "*Wo ist der Mann aus Amerika?*" Where is the American guy? I wonder what he needs and suddenly tire of the rudeness. I tell Barbara I will meet them in Spain if she will give me the details. No need. She tells me that Lisbeth, a Danish girl who handles the ad agency trip plans when they're in Europe, will call with all the information about my ticket and flights and hotel. Lisbeth will arrange everything. Lisbeth will take care of it.

$\mathscr{R}$ I C H

Wilhelm had no sense of taste. Literally, he was old and could not taste anything he ate. Ib Sølvhøj, Wilhelm's son and my father-in-law, did have a fine sense of taste and loved the best wines and food. I was the cook, and we had an evening in Jutland without the women. Ib and I had gone pheasant hunting that morning, my first such venture, and I shot three birds. We would have them for supper. I remember the recipe, so simple, and we joked that Wilhelm would judge the cooking, perfect, since he could not taste.

We needed butter, shallots, garlic, a touch of brandy, and heavy cream. And the pheasants, cleaned and quartered.

I sautéed the pheasant first, in the butter. Turned the pieces once, sprinkled shallots and garlic around the pan, scraped and moved the pieces, put the lid on for a bit, and when the pheasant was nearly done, deglazed the pan with the brandy, let it burn a moment, and added the cream. I reduced the brandy and cream sauce and finished it all with a few pieces of cold butter.

The sauce had a creamy sheen, spooned again over the pheasant. I do not remember if we had rice or potatoes or just bread with the pheasant. But I remember the dinner table, the silence, a bite of food, the looks, testing again, another look and another bite of food. Then Wilhelm laughed out loud, and then Ib, and then we all laughed, looking at Wilhelm, tears in his eyes. Wilhelm leaned back and laughed again, "*Det smager sgu' godt, du!*" By God, that tastes good!

A simple recipe, the perfect judge, tested in Jutland.

RICH OR POOR

I've never been poor. I've owed money, or spent down to nothing, or had to take a night job, but I've never been poor. We were raised as if we were poor. We ate at home and when on the road, we read the right-hand side of the menu, where the price was, and worked our way to the left-hand side, which had the dishes and the descriptions. We bought things only when absolutely necessary, a TV only when we shamed our family by watching through the neighbors' window.

When I returned from Europe, I had run my savings dry. I was setting up a household for my Danish wife and her child, and I worked three jobs: substitute teaching five days a week in the daytime, and six evenings a week at Duke's in the mall, making food and serving up steaks and such to the late-evening and night crowds. From Duke's I would go to a Manpower office temp job, proofreading the text of training manuals. I remember the microfiche screens scrolling down and waking abruptly, having fallen asleep for a moment or a minute. But I wasn't poor; I was just running behind and catching up.

The true riches I have experienced are about opportunity and grace. I have received jobs in the last moment, calls to travel, offers of employment, promises of support, unexpected bequests, and gifts beyond measure. I have never feared the morrow, despite not knowing how things could ever work out. Rich. Not poor. God's blessings.

BÉARNAISE AT ALKENHØJ

It was a nostalgic evening at Alkenhøj, comfortable and friendly; we had eaten well, the usual at Alkenhøj, and we were satisfied. But for me, nothing could mask my persistent sense of regret and loss, the failures and lost Danish dreams, opportunities, and adventures of the past decade. I was on a brief summer visit from Milwaukee, just before beginning my new job as principal at Vincent High School. I had left Denmark three years before, missed it almost painfully, and wondered every day if I had made the right decision to leave.

Henning, Christian, and I sat around a campfire in the yard a short distance from the farmhouse. We poked sticks in the embers, and Henning asked about the meal I had prepared. That was part of the nostalgia, as I had cooked for a living in Denmark, and for three years around the time Lisbeth and I parted, I was køkkenchef in Tivoli Gardens in Copenhagen. I had even catered Lisbeth's wedding to Hasse, and this evening at Alkenhøj I prepared the same béarnaise that was our signature sauce in Tivoli. It was rich, and very good.

"What's the sauce made of?" Henning asked. We had finished it off, and I remembered he had eaten the last of it with a spoon, warm, right from the serving pot.

"Béarnaise. Egg yolks, butter, tarragon, and a little reduced vinegar. Sometimes a little pepper, or salt, depending on if it's unsalted butter."

"No, I mean what is the sauce part of it? Not the flavoring. Like chicken stock, or broth, or milk, water, or what?"

"Well, a few egg yolks, and mostly butter," I said.

"No, I mean the bulk, the liquid, the sauce...what we ate, not what it tasted like." He sounded impatient; frustrated, maybe, that I had forgotten my Danish. I remembered again he had been eating the sauce with a spoon after we finished the burgers for which the sauce was intended.

"*Smør*," I said. "Butter. Smør!"

"Smør," he said. "Butter. Nothing else?"

"Melted butter, egg yolks to draw it together, splash of tarragon vinegar to flavor."

"How much butter?" he asked. "How much butter did we eat?"

"A kilo and a half. Maybe a bit more, with what was on the plate in the fridge."

He was excited—sounded almost scared. "A kilo and a half of butter. We were only six people. The kids didn't eat any. Nothing left over!" I remembered his spoon, at the end.

"Right, Henning. Pretty rich stuff."

B É A R N A I S E — *R* E C I P E

For an evening's service:

Two to three ladles pasteurized egg yolks; add
Half ladle tarragon vinegar reduction.
Whisk over very low heat in enameled cast iron pot until thick and smooth.
Remove from heat, whisk in steady thin stream
Five kilograms melted butter or best-quality margarine, no dregs; add
Chopped tarragon, pepper, and salt to taste.

Hold near heat, whisk in warm water if too thick.

Serve sauce as side with carved beef roast, steaks, best burgers.

ℳISE EN ℘LACE

Anthony Bourdain's take on *mise en place* is correct, for the most, even if he doesn't utilize the notion outside the kitchen. It pervades all, or should. But I remember a summer Sunday evening in Tivoli during which the question of order, preparation, adequate stockpiles of ingredients, and follow-through went totally wrong.

The restaurants—Bernstorff, on the street side, and Paraplyen, in the Gardens—took part in the nationwide tourist board promotion called *DanMenu*. Forty-eight kroner for a two-course dinner, a different menu for each night of the week, a single dish each night. Sunday was Wiener schnitzel, the most popular of our offerings, and it was a quality offering. Freshly cut boneless veal steaks, trimmed, sliced, pounded thin with a heavy mallet, and breaded. These were sautéed in butter, together with hand-cut new potatoes, and served with green peas, ordinary frozen green peas, simply warmed up by blanching in a strainer in gently boiling water. Out on the plate and done.

We served between two and three hundred of these on a Sunday evening in the two restaurants, and as chef I was always there, and a cook did most of the work. I remember leaving the kitchen during a lull in the traffic to make a phone call upstairs. I told Niels, the cook, to send for me if he had any problem. The cooks would never do this; despite being much younger than me, they were formally trained, and

I was a foreigner who had learned some tricks of the trade, was a good organizer, and had hired them all, but didn't know the craft as they did (or supposed they did). They usually told me, in good enough humor, to get out of the way and let them do the cooking.

Sunday was an easier day, as most of the orders would be the schnitzel. I went to make the call and didn't hear any shout for help, so took my time and returned perhaps fifteen or twenty minutes later. I walked into the kitchen and stopped. True shock. Niels had a rush going and was furiously sautéing at the stove, five of the six burners in full use, large sauté pans. And plates everywhere around the kitchen, on the counters, beside the dishwasher, the prep tables, along the stove, and in the service hallway. Probably forty or fifty plates with schnitzel and potatoes, some piping hot, just finished, but most of them cooling and losing their crispy edge to time and temperature. No peas in sight.

"*Niels, hva' fanden laver du?*" What in the devil's name are you doing?

"Ran out of peas," was his only answer as he kept on cooking. He had no one to run to the freezer to get more and wouldn't stop to get them himself or lower himself to shout for me to come and help. Pure clash of *mise* and pride! And pride won out.

THE BOOKSTORE,
COPENHAGEN, 1979

I am on the second floor of the bookstore. It's a good place to wait, halfway between the train station and the walking street, where maybe we'll shop for something, talk, and wander a bit. I'm early, to be sure Lisbeth won't have to wait. It's a good day, feeling proud and confident, more success at *KISS*, the intensive language school in the heart of Copenhagen. I've moved up another of the thirteen steps, don't have to retake the level I've been on for three or four weeks—lessons three days a week, five hours a day, as much time at home doing repetitions. Most students have to redo most levels at least once. Not me.

I don't speak English much to anyone any more, and I'm getting good at this difficult and obscure language. I have new plans to quit my work teaching English in night school. English as a foreign language. Foreign. I'll take any job I can manage in Danish. This is my adventure, living in Europe, not a tourist, not a visitor, not even an American.

I don't think Lisbeth likes my Danish much; it makes me a different person, not so smart, awkward at best. We'll talk about it when she gets to the bookstore. Probably in English. We'll talk about the restaurant job I may have, assistant manager at Peder Oxe on Gråbrødrestorvet: "the Gray Brothers Square," I know now, named for the monks who used to live there.

The bookstore is a good place to wait. The second floor has a café counter. We can order a sandwich or walk and find someplace else. Also, the bookstore's second floor windows look out on the street below, and I'll be able to see Lisbeth when she comes. Walking my way. From Nørreport Station. I have coffee and study my lesson, level three repetitions: "That's a pretty notebook…a green notebook…a new notebook… your sister's notebook."

It's ten minutes after, no, twenty, and my coffee's no longer hot, not really warm even. Time moves slowly, as it has ever since we arrived in Denmark. Lisbeth's homecoming, my adventure. A reflection of her year with me in the United States. It had been her dream to move to the States. I taught college, had an educated job, and she couldn't find work except as a waitress or nurse's aide. Her nursing papers didn't qualify her for proud work. Now in Denmark, my papers were good enough, but a strange and difficult language blocked the way. My adventure. "Is that your notebook? Your sister's notebook? Your green notebook?" And I wasn't as smart as I used to be.

At first Lisbeth defended me, as I had done for her in the States. When I applied for work at the Kommune's employment office, they told me I didn't qualify for unemployment payments. When Lisbeth heard this, she got her coat, stormed out, and attacked like a mama bear, telling them her man didn't want money, but a job. I was her man, her big American. No handouts needed. So they got me a job, aide in a day care center, since I had been a teacher. Didn't last long, little children having no way to get their point across to the tall man who talked funny, but this gave me time to search for a job teaching English. Which turned out to be worse than the day care. Night school teaching assignments through the political unions, dreary drizzly Danish winter evenings, long train rides home, lonely. So I planned to learn the language, a chance to work. I am getting closer, level three out of thirteen. "Is that your notebook?"

A half hour. Lisbeth will come walking, striding, soon. Maybe when I learn the language, get a good job, we can get a car. Lisbeth thinks that's a bad idea. Most everyone we know takes the bus or train, rides a bicycle. Or walks. We'll get a car. We have our apartment finally. Months on a waiting list. We live in Langhuset. At one time the longest residential building in all of Europe. Langhuset. My Danish is good enough to know this reads exactly "*the* long house." Concrete panels. Gray. Nearly three-quarters of a mile long, fifty or sixty four-story walk-ups. Each time I come around the tree line from the train station and look down our apartment block, I can barely make out a person standing at our entrance door. Forty-fifth entrance. We are third floor on the left. Our home. Inside, cozy and hopeful. Outside, raw concrete. Bicycle racks.

I pack up my papers from school, wait in silence, and begin to think about heading home. Maybe something's happened. I got to the book store early enough that she could not have come and gone before I arrived. She would have left a message. Maybe. I feel less confident, and the happy feeling about success at school and prospects for a good job has turned to something else. And as so often, just as I begin to lose faith, I see Lisbeth coming down the block. Athletic, walking fast, heading my way. Almost an hour late, no matter. I hope everything is all right, but she has a look on her face as if she's thinking about something far off, inconsequential. At least she's OK, she's here. We can talk. Walk.

I stand and lean toward the window as she approaches. I watch her step to the door below. She stops at a book rack outside the door, takes a book from the display, and opens it. I watch as she shuffles through the pages, replaces the book on the rack. And takes another. This one she reads for several minutes, turning the pages slowly.

$\mathcal{B}$REAKFAST AT $\mathcal{K}$ØDBYEN

I love breakfast anyway. The food is simple, and it's a hopeful start to the day. I took knives to the meat-cutting and processing center in the industrial outskirts of Copenhagen. Kødbyen. *Kød* means "meat," and *byen* means "the city." The meat city. A hundred butchers and processors, restaurant and kitchen supply houses. I was still køkkenchef at Paraplyen in Tivoli Gardens, and usually the butcher picked up the cooks' knives for sharpening and returned them the next day or so. But this day I went myself, and I think it had to do with knives. It was a sunny day. I could hear the sound of sharpening machines, the grinding wheels, on the second floor of Larsen's kitchen supply shop, the one we used. Pots and pans, clothing, knives. Today I stopped at the small lunch counter restaurant at the entrance to the complex.

Two eggs, fried; a thick piece of French bread, hand-sliced, soft, not toasted; a thin slice of Esrom cheese; and strong coffee. I sat at the counter and wondered at my good fortune. This must have been some sort of a half day off, as I was not hurrying and somewhat lonely. Perhaps I had gone to Larsen's just to look at knives. But I was alone, nothing to do, and the eggs, the bread and cheese, and the coffee were a comfort.

"*Tak ska' du ha'*," thank you, and I went about my day. Into the street.

$\mathcal{C}$ A R E

I pretended not to care when I learned that Lisbeth had a lover. When it became too obvious and when proof collided with my too-busy schedule at work, I confronted her, and after a day or so told her "him or me," and if him, go, leave. I think I knew that I would have to be the one to go, ultimately, but I put the blame on her and showed that it was her choice and that my wishes weren't part of it, if I truly had any. I must have showed too clearly that I didn't have any feelings that could be stronger than her own, for me or for him. I never told her if or that I was hurt or sorry or in any sort of pain. So, I pretended that I didn't care, and time told the tale that I did in fact care, one way or another. I began to see her in town, in the city, from behind or in a crowd or in the train station, and each time, it turned out not to be her. A day in the spring, in true Danish style, she asked if I would cater her wedding to her new guy, and trying desperately to be Scandinavian, I agreed. A hundred people ate well, drank good wine, and Lisbeth tried to introduce me to a new girl, also named Lisbeth, who lived in Copenhagen, and my closest friends kept asking if I was OK, and I pretended I was. Three years later, at my farmhouse in Jutland, on Bønfeldtvej, I told her exactly how I felt, that I missed her so and that it just plain hurt so badly. And I cried. I did not pretend I was hurt, but I may have been fooling myself, again.

$\mathscr{W}$ E $\mathscr{S}$ L E P T $\mathscr{O}$ U T S I D E

We didn't sleep outside; we slept in the car. But it felt like outside, free. The car was her home anyway, and I thought it was a fantastic adventure and wanted to join up. We slept in the car, outside, in Yosemite, beautiful, deep blue-green, quiet, still, dripping. Will we marry? Waiting to capture the moment, be a gypsy. I ate fire now; she taught me in the clown class. Proud, another notch on my gun handle. I did the project and spent the weekend in San Francisco, without money, eating out of dumpsters and in soup kitchens, and the class sat quiet, one girl cried, and I told of the loneliness and the walking, cold. Sleeping in the car was a dream.

We slept in the car, washed in the park restrooms, ate sandwiches, and she answered my question about marriage.

She said, "Why don't we get tattoos instead?" Maybe flames, for fire eating. We drove to the city and found a tattoo parlor. I need to tell you about this. We arrived, looked at drawings, and then waited when three drunks stumbled in and arranged for one of them to have his forehead tattooed. "Hey, forehead OK?"

"If I can reach it, I can tattoo it."

The three fumbled with ideas for the tattoo, and then, "Never too Old to Love," in crude block letters. Forehead. A warning.

$\mathcal{K}$NIFE, $\mathcal{T}$HREE $\mathcal{D}$OLLARS, $\mathcal{S}$AN $\mathcal{F}$RANCISCO, 1983

When I went to San Francisco, I took along three dollars, enough to buy the knife. It was a separate project, not really related to the weekend living on the streets with no money. So I had cheated the project from the start, though I wasn't going to use the money for food or entertainment or travel. The deal was, I would buy a round-trip ticket to San Francisco from Berkeley. I would leave for the city on Friday afternoon and return Sunday evening. No money, no change of clothes, no reading material or supplies, nothing, and try to manage as homeless, wandering, gather food however I could manage.

This was a personal project for a clown ministry class at the Pacific School of Religion. I was in love with the fire-eating clown ministry professor-lady who lived in her car and traveled the country, storytelling and eating fire. She approved the project and wished me well for the weekend. Be safe. But I took along three dollars for a pocket knife I happened to have seen in the window of a sporting goods store on an earlier trip to the city. I do not remember the motivation to buy the knife—for safety or because it looked nifty or because it was simply the decision whether or not to buy it, which I didn't.

But the project was compromised, because I could buy a meal or soap or whatever if I wanted to or had to, and the project was compromised.

I did not buy the knife, and I did not include the weekend-long debate as to whether or not to buy it in the project report. Nor did I spend the money on anything else, as there was plenty of money to be found on the street, with the time I had to scan the areas under and around vending machines and pay phones. Nor did I give the money to anyone, despite the endless opportunities.

Food was plenteous, in plain view in fast-food restaurants and do-nut shops, outside back doors to kitchens, in dumpsters, and on top of garbage cans. Likewise, a caring town afforded many soup kitchens and free samples, and the days and nights were spent moving to keep warm and safe, searching for loose change and opportunity, and I did not buy the knife.

$\mathcal{O}$ V E R

We had the small flame tattoos and time to think it over. We spoke on the telephone for months, Copenhagen to America, but she came anyway. She was a clown, a professional, an ordained minister and storyteller, and I don't know if she still slept in her car. But she flew to Copenhagen, and it was the end. Or perhaps she was visiting friends in Germany. And took a side trip to Denmark.

She was suddenly loud and crude. She spoke no Danish, of course, but challenged passers-by with her clown antics. I was proud of my Danish and my understanding of local decorum, and she betrayed my private treasure of the language. One day, on a crowded city bus, she shouted to the riders, "Do you know why I love this man? I love this man…" and I don't remember the rest. My memory of her is blocked from that moment. In a moment of curiosity years later, I looked her up on the Internet. No mention, no record, gone. Even her name was missing. It was over.

$\mathcal{D}$ IFFERENT $\mathcal{T}$ IMES

I have never needed chocolate or alcohol, as the prompt directs, but I have needed cigarettes and coffee. I have gone to bed late at night, dreaming of the first cigarette and cup of coffee in the morning. Morning solitude was never really that, as three or four cigarettes kept me company as the coffee brewed, or a drive down the road to town held the promise of a café or a newspaper and friendly waitress. My cup of coffee, perhaps the fifth or sixth today, is on the table. My friend. Cigarettes were too obviously destructive, and I quit many times, off and on since age sixteen, finally quit at forty-six, the slow death too obvious.

While I have never needed alcohol or chocolate, I have a compulsive lonely habit, needing a companion to make up for the loneliness. I have had an addictive relationship with nicotine, with caffeine, and with loneliness. My friends and family in Denmark used hashish, a gentle evening-closer on the farm at Alkenhøj. I lived down the road, had toyed with the idea of becoming part of the collective, but it was clear that I was not built for it, didn't have the easy temperament. Even so, I was a regular guest at the farm, and the evenings were slow and warm, one channel of state television, high quality and thoughtful. Coffee in the blue enamel drip pot, heavy cream, and hash. A round and again, easy.

Turning forty: I dreaded the day. My greatest life's accomplishment, learning Danish well enough to teach refugees in the country, turning to loneliness, farmhouse on an isolated country road to nowhere, no chance any person would stumble on my existence. I sat in my kitchen, coffee, no alcohol, knowing that if I stayed in the country I would become first comfortable, then compulsive, then addictive. With loneliness, coffee, cigarettes, hashish. I heard that my family and friends were coming with a birthday cake. I ran for my van, drove off to avoid them, but passed them on the way and had to turn around and share the occasion. My house was sold within a month, my bags packed, lived at the farm while papers were completed, and I left the country for good.

TURNING FORTY— JUTLAND, DENMARK

Turning forty was depressing. I hid at the house, alone, but then someone called and told me a small crowd from Alkenhøj was coming to throw me a birthday party. I couldn't manage this, and anyway, I had decided enough was enough. I pulled on shoes and grabbed my keys and went out to the truck, to get away before the birthday party arrived. Old Hanomag van, hand brush-painted dull gray delivery truck, my only escape for the past two years, an American's dream in Denmark, to have wheels, freedom. I drove back along my dead-end road toward Astrup and passed the Alkenhøj party coming in the opposite direction. I was too late. They honked and waved, and I turned around, followed them back along the lonely road, toward my house. My house.

I lived in Jutland, the Danish mainland, rolling farmland, maybe like Iowa or Kansas would be to someone from New York. People kept to themselves, tended the land, their houses, their families. And I was the American, the American who lived in old Dagny Laursen's house. It didn't matter to the local folks that I had bought the house from Fru Laursen, who was moving the five miles to Astrup, age convincing her she had to live in town.

I remodeled the house, gutting the stale and musty innards of the small, whitewashed fieldstone and mortar dwelling. It was two or three hundred years old, a typical Danish farmhouse, but I tried to make it my house. I did the cement and carpentry work myself, new floorboards, cinderblock and stucco inner walls, painted white, put in bigger windows and a fresh woodstove. Wood slat ceilings, following the contours of sagging rafters. The L-shaped building connected to the barn and stable, cows and pigs in years past. I found rats in the dug well and got the town water line extended a mile to the house, the last house on the road. I had chickens in the yard, a couple of roosters, and a cat, my only companions.

My ex-brother-in-law Henning, who was part of the collective farm, Alkenhøj, ten miles away, past Astrup, reminded me often that no pretty girls would be coming down this road. He was right. Only once did a girl stop in, a distant neighbor's daughter, said she had run out of gas on her moped. She looked around the house while I called her father and said I would bring her and the motorbike home in my van. Maybe she did run out of gas, but I think she was just curious. She was plain and anxious. Henning was correct about the girls who might stop in.

This was another turning point in my life, turning forty only part of it, but it was different and painful. I had been divorced from Lisbeth for nearly four years and had moved to Jutland from Copenhagen to be away from her while staying close to her family, who lived nearby: Lisbeth's sisters and their menfolk, and her father and mother, who I admired, all of them. Trying to stay in touch, I guess, but the page had been turned, and there was no way to remain close, no option. Turning forty seemed like a hopelessly lost past, an out-of-focus and dismal future.

Lisbeth visited once, that year, and for the first time I cried openly, standing with her in my farmhouse kitchen, tears, asking why it had come to this, how had it happened? Her visit was brief, stopping just to say hello. It had been four years, she was remarried, and I was in Jutland. My last cooking job in Copenhagen had been to cater her wedding, and I now taught my nearly fluent Danish language skills to angry and frightened Palestinian and Kurdish refugees assigned to our Jutland county offices.

This was the end of my ten-year adventure, the flight from Muhlenberg College, from Holly, from family, Phil and Gena, and from so many commonplace golden opportunities. I was forty, the afternoon birthday party with Henning and the Alkenhøj bunch was quiet and reflective, and they left after a while to resume their family comforts and responsibilities. I confirmed the mind's decision in my heart that day, laid plans that night to sell the house and leave Denmark. I was the American staying briefly in Dagny Laursen's house; the heavy walls and the silent, dead-end road framed my future there.

So I determined to leave, and within a month had made all the arrangements, sold the house, and moved into my van. Parked at Alkenhøj for the several weeks as I closed out obligations at work. I built a sturdy wooden chest in the workshop at Alkenhøj and packed it with the few and most precious pieces of relationships and travels and projects from those years. The plan was to fly to the States, spend some weeks with my mother and father in Virginia, buy a car, and drive to Jack and Helene MacConnell's at their mountain cabin in Pennsylvania, and then head west to Milwaukee, a promise of a place to stay with an old Muhlenberg College colleague and his wife who lived there, look for work, cooking or teaching, anything, and start over.

Start over, turning forty. It didn't feel hopeful, felt more like dying, like death. The decade had begun as an adventure, full of energy and promise and dreams. And now it felt like a hole was opening up in the road ahead. I felt already that it would be a painful and difficult job just to climb out of that hole. I don't remember wondering if I would not fall too far, or for too long.

$\mathscr{P}$AIR OF $\mathscr{V}$ISITS, $\mathscr{S}$HOES

I remember shopping in Tangier, Morocco, for anything, really, something to take home, something local and exotic. We bargained for everything, it seemed, and it was a great opportunity. I was on my second trip to North Africa, and I felt more confident with Susse than when I had been there with my father, timid in all things foreign. Why did we ever travel from the easygoing parts of Spain to the hectic press of Tangier? But I was going to buy something special, and I needed a pair of sandals, so we looked. Camelhide shoes, boots, and found one shoe of a pair of unusual and truly foreign sandals, perfect, but tied to another, much smaller sandal.

The man who owned the cramped shop started at a high and unreasonable price, and we began to bargain the price down while he looked for the matching shoe of the pair. I tried on the one, size 45, but the one tied to it was another size, much smaller. We bickered on the price, and I liked the shoe, hoping he'd find the other of the pair, now a fair enough price, and I was tiring of the banter. No second shoe, and I wondered if someone else had a pair of off-sized shoes, a 45 he had never tried on, with his own perfect 37, left satisfied, arrived home to disappointment.

"OK, half price only one shoe fit," said the man.

"Half price."

We stared at each other. I did not dare laugh. I did not know.

$\mathcal{L}$AST $\mathcal{C}$HANCE, $\mathcal{K}$OH $\mathcal{S}$AMET

I believe in special moments and last chances. Mr. Visith ran up, out of breath. "Come quick, Mister Scott. Need help!" It had been a restful evening. Koh Samet was an out-of-the-way Thai island, seldom frequented by foreigners, and my two-dollar-per-night bamboo hut was part of a primitive corner of paradise. On my way home to the United States, Copenhagen's Tivoli Gardens season over, I chose to take the long way home this year, in no real hurry. I had been in Thailand for nearly a month. Koh Samet was a welcome relief from the trash and noise of Bangkok.

Mr. Visith, a retired army colonel who owned the place, looked scared, out of character for him. "Come quick, man drunk and crazy, the guards going to shoot him!" The guards. I had seen them along the beach, mean-looking, local order. I wondered why Mr. Visith needed me. "Englishman, in water! There! Won't stop." Mr. Visith pointed, and I could hear shouting, curses, howling. He ran ahead.

I passed the two security men, one in army fatigues with an old, long-barreled shotgun, best for goose. The other guard wore shorts and a T-shirt, but held a slick, automatic rifle, pointing it at the man in the water twenty or thirty yards out, knee-deep in the low surf. The T-shirt guard shouted angry words, waved the gun. "Shut up, or I shoot!" I did not see Mr. Visith.

"OK, OK, one minute!"

"No one minute! Too loud, drunk, bad!"

"OK." I waded into the water. The man howled and cursed.

"Bastards stole my money, passport, everything! What am I gonna do?"

He was Irish, heavy accent, angry, drunk, howling. I had seen him playing cards with some local Thai boys earlier.

"Stole my wallet, everything. Off the table, sons of bitches!"

"You've got to shut up and get off the beach. It's their island. They're really angry and they're going to shoot."

"I don't care," he moaned, "what am I gonna do?"

He cursed and cried, and the guards shouted some quick words, waving me away from the Irishman.

"Hang on." The Irishman lurched and cursed, louder.

Quietly, "OK, friend, listen to me. I'm leaving you now, and then the guards are going to shoot you. They are going to kill you." He took a quick breath.

I walked away from him, to the side, and carefully away from the guards. The Irishman whimpered softly, "What am I gonna do?"

I repeated once, quietly, "They will shoot you now."

I heard one of the guns clack, cocked. I walked onto the beach and away. No sound. There was no shot this night. Just the endless return of soft waves. Paradise.

CHE BRIDGE, MILWAUKEE, 1987

Bob Jasna, the principal, stood in the doorway, third-floor computer lab. He nodded his head at me, wanted to talk in the hall. We were in a reading exercise on the screens, students listening while the lab teacher directed. Neither the children nor I were particularly interested in the lesson, but the special help period was a break in the day; we got to go to the third floor, and it was bright and open. Our usual room was in the basement. Even nicer to be called into the hall. Something was up.

I was the English teacher in what they called the Ninth Grade Family, four teachers chosen for their patient and generally fair dealings with the thirty or so toughest ninth graders in the school. At-risk. All of us. It wasn't a real family, as all four teachers were white and all were male, and our kids were the difficult, mostly black girls and boys arriving each morning in yellow buses from their neighborhoods. Their presence created a contradiction in Milwaukee's once-prestigious Riverside University High School, gang signs in every out-of-the-way spot in the school or courtyard, lots of wasted time in the school. Broken glass in the courtyard, where students smoked freely after lunch.

But this was a permanent job, after a year substitute teaching in the city. I had made enough of a name for myself, never turning down an assignment, even in the most difficult situations. Other subs refused calls to any of the notoriously dangerous schools. The advantage to subbing in the more frightening schools was not being responsible for anything except keeping order, which I seemed to be able to do in the classrooms and cafeterias and halls.

When Bob Jasna asked for help, often it was for what one of the assistant principals called "roto-rooting," going to the top floor of the building and sweeping down the stairwells, picking up students or outsiders loitering or skipping class, taking them to detention, or putting them out. Mr. Jasna was nothing like my stereotypical image of a high school principal. He was tall and well dressed, intelligent, and articulate. And he was tough when need be.

"Morgan, can you help us out?" That question usually meant class coverage, or extra help in the cafeteria, doing something without extra pay. It was early in the day. Maybe someone had gone home sick. In any case, it was easy to help, as it meant a break in the daily routine of the Ninth Grade Family. I said I'd be glad to help, and Mr. Jasna told the lab teacher she'd be working alone for a time.

In the hall, he told me.

"We have a problem and thought you could help us. There's a dead body in the river and the kids are hearing about it, and I need you to direct traffic on the bridge."

He explained, the traffic was not cars on the bridge, but students slipping out of the school to see what was going on. We walked quickly to his office. I wasn't sure how I could really help. I had no problem pushing unwilling students with grammar and writing exercises in class, or watching for trouble in the cafeteria, but the excitement of a dead body in the river and a crowd of loose teenagers might be too much.

I was generally competent as a teacher, but Mr. Jasna was asking me to do work reserved for administrators, who so often were former coaches, shop teachers and driver education teachers, often loud and crude and unkind. I thought of them, the principals, the disciplinarians, as out-of-breath, impatient men with whistles, pointing, shouting, lining kids up, hurrying them along, or stopping them in their tracks, making them wait. I taught English, had taught education courses in college, and never for even a moment imagined doing the work of a principal in a big-city high school. I wasn't confident.

I told Mr. Jasna that I would be glad to help. I had no idea how quickly and uneventfully this would become the first day of my new life, now connected in the river to the end of another person's life. Bob Jasna handed me a radio, a walkie-talkie, palm size, with a short antenna. It fit smoothly in my hand and felt just right. He showed me the single push-to-talk button and the volume control. We walked out the door into the sunlight. I could hear excited students at the windows above us, all four floors.

"Morgan, I want you to go down and keep the kids off the bridge. DiDonato will watch up here, but if any of them make it down to you, you send them back. Or if they come across the bridge from downtown, be sure to move them along up here. Just keep them off the bridge. You OK with this?"

"Yes, I'm fine."

I walked fast the hundred yards to the bridge and turned, checking my territory and planning my defense or escape. A car or two passed, people staring to see what was going on. I could see a police boat in the river, but I never saw the body, never looked. I was not curious. It was a bright and sunny day, and the light breeze felt fresh.

I could see Bob Jasna standing at the door, pointing toward me, talking with Mr. DiDonato, one of the four assistant principals in the school. I appreciated them for their confidence in me, and as they talked together, they looked competent. They were in charge of a difficult situation, reasonable. They were in control. The radio crackled, startled me. I pressed the button. "Yes?" I released and waited.

"You OK? Got a couple of boys coming across the bridge."

"Yes, OK." I waited for the students on the bridge's sidewalk.

"Hey, Phenix. What's going on? Saw the police cars down the street."

"Don't rightly know, but you got to get up to the school."

"What's the rush?" Not particularly friendly, and not ready to go along with the request. I pressed the radio's button, and it crackled.

"You OK?" It was DiDonato.

I pointed the stubby antenna at the boys and raised my eyebrows.

"We OK, gentlemen?"

Friendly, reasonable, in charge. Competent. Confident. This was the first day of my new life. I played no particularly important part in the day, an unknown person died, the school was short on help, the sun was bright, there was a fresh wind, and the students moved on.

"Yes. OK, Mr. DiDonato."

"Thanks, Morgan." It was Bob Jasna.

$\mathcal{C}$OWARDICE

I knew I was going to suffer, but I went ahead anyway. I stood at the altar. It was a Lutheran church, because Angela's Catholic church would not accept the annulment I had obtained over Lisbeth's protest. Angela was divorced anyway. It was a mess, and unnecessary. I knew it was the wrong thing, and there wasn't even an adventure in it, like when Holly and I ran off to marry, or when Europe and Lisbeth conspired and tantalized my mind.

To make matters worse, my father and mother were present, and my father had offered to share in officiating. I was standing across from my father and a pastor I do not remember. My father was always capable of gearing up for even the worst choice, providing intellectual justification for this union. But I was forty-one or forty-two and should have known better.

I listened as my father spoke, and we stood an arm's length away. I could have reached out to him and simply said, "Please save me, Father." It would have been biblical and something no one would have forgotten, ever. And I would have saved myself and so many others the heartache and plain old bother of a bad choice. Angela would call it her very bad choice; I am certain now that she was correct.

But I went ahead anyway, and I knew I was going to suffer.

ℐHE 𝒫RICE OF ℒAND

It was July, 1990 and it was over. In my heart, clearly. In fact, we both must have known it was over. The thought was small and quiet, growing, but the words were shouted in the car at sixty miles an hour, heading to Wisconsin lake country. Angela: "No one is going to buy any land today!"

And me: "If I want to buy land, I'll buy land!" I was driving, and she was along as a witness. We had separate professions, separate budgets, separate dreams, and now, separate journeys, threatening and diverging and sparring.

The land was an escape, a triangle of thatch undergrowth on a shallow end of a small lake in Adams County, north of Madison and several hours from Milwaukee, where we lived. It was an unhandy location, but everything about it said we were finished as a couple, and that was OK. Angela was a first-rate lawyer, torts and on the verge of criminal defense practice. Friends said she was a shark, and she knew how to attack. The question of a land purchase was not a matter of discussion or compromise or countering dreams; it was block, strangle, and destroy. "No land."

I bought the land, and only months later offered it at half the price to the agent who had sold it to us, as part of our divorce settlement. I signed off on every demand and request. Maybe I won every point; I had my freedom, and bought land in Virginia instead. It was over.

MERCY

I believe in mercy. I wasn't family. I didn't know what having a percentage of Vegas meant, and I didn't know who "the boys" were. I knew my new wife's family owned a Milwaukee supper club, got free tickets to Packers games and the Super Bowl. I had married Angela a year after I came to town, wedding reception at the family restaurant. I found a job in the school system and gained promotions. But I wasn't really family.

When the senior George Bush visited Italian Fest at the Milwaukee lakefront on his second campaign trail, they cleared the crowds in the lakefront park, and the president stopped at the family restaurant's sausage stand. News photographers stood behind a fence. I was moving sausages on the grill, helping out with Angela's cousins, Johnny and Joey, and President Bush leaned over and asked me if the sausages were something special. "Sure, local, Glorioso's. The best. Do you want one?" He laughed and moved on, but a picture of the president and me talking, Angela's cousins Johnny and Joey working in the background, landed on the front page of the *New York Times*. I think Johnny and Joey were upset. I would have been. The restaurant was family, and I wasn't.

All the News
t's Fit to Print"

The New York Tin

XXVII . . . . No. 47,575   Copyright © 1988 The New York Times   NEW YORK, SATURDAY, JULY 23, 1988

Bush Courts Votes in Milwaukee and New Jersey   Associated Press
Vice President Bush being served eggs and Italian sausage at an Italian festival in Milwaukee yesterday before going on to New Jersey. He said support of ethnic voters would be based on values, not heritage. Page 9.

That fall, Angela's father, Joe, had heart surgery. Weak, he fought for his life. We waited outside his room, and just two at a time could go in and visit, family only. Laurie, Joe's blonde girlfriend of many years waited also. Laurie cried softly for Joe, and cried because she was not allowed in. She was not family, and there were hard feelings over parts of the past they didn't share; the years had not softened the hardest feelings. I was sure that Laurie's tears were real, and I was not part of that family story. Angela and her sister came from their father's room. "Let's go, Laurie."

"But it says family only."

"I can take you in. We're family."

The waiting room fell silent, and we walked through the doors. Joe lay in the bed, tubes and monitors, but held Laurie's hand, looked up, shrugged.

"Thanks." He did not die.

Christmas came, and Joe wrapped a present for me, a gun from his own collection, a vintage deer rifle. Silence, as I opened the obvious present.

"Thanks for bringing Laurie in at the hospital."

I was not family. Angela and I argued a lot about many things; I wandered off on ventures with country land and old trucks, and we divorced that year. I moved out to a hotel downtown and looked down alleys when I got out of my car. When I left town, I did not return.

I believe in mercy. I am grateful to have received so much in return for having given so little.

$\mathscr{P}$ROMISES

I've kept my promise, but not always, and I find myself looking over my shoulder from time to time, remembering. Partly shame, partly regret, but mostly just not keeping my word. I was reminded a few weeks ago. Of course I knew that half of marriages in the United States, or more than half, ended in divorce. Half is an easy and simple concept to accept.

Several weeks ago I met with a student working on her dissertation, and she cited statistics in her study indicating that 495 of every thousand marriages ended in divorce. That's about half of all marriages, but 495 sounded like quite a crowd of faces, nearly a thousand different people, as there are two in each marriage. A thousand people in all those failed marriages, a thousand people, gone or cast off, devastated, relieved or bitter, shocked, worn out, or in tears. A thousand failures. Not to mention damaged children, angry parents, helpless pets, and family and friends and lawyers, ministers and judges, and possessions of all kinds. Certainly disappointments, far cries from the original expressions of joy, the energetic starting points, fresh agreements to join and travel together. The promises. I recall them all.

I remember that my marriages had the usual, basic features on the way in, perhaps as many features as those that describe the reasons the marriages didn't last. But I believe that the expectation in each, or at least the hope, was for success and permanency, an exclusive and final future. And I would bet that if one could tally the statistics on how many people willingly agree to the terms of a marriage, and count on the marriage lasting forever, the figure would approach 100 percent, a thousand marriages out of a thousand. Two thousand people planning and trusting and hoping, against the odds.

So, a marriage is a decision, personal; it's an agreement, between two. A marriage is also a public promise, seldom made in private, so it's an agreement among many. And even in the most private circumstances, a witness is required, sharing and sealing the promise. More critically, the agreement and promise almost always carry the weight of contract, or law, and the marriage is therefore more easily entered into than dissolved. Finally, the promise to marry so often includes a sacred vow, involving the witness to the words by an all-knowing Creator—in any case, a being that supersedes human limitations and frailties. This last piece of the marriage promise must have some devastating effect on an individual's long-term prospects within the hearing of an all-powerful and potentially vengeful God. I have glanced over my shoulder, wondering about just this, in the midst of a wedding's hope and anticipation. But now, I am confident that God has always known my promises were in vain, as soon as they were spoken. Before I knew, He knew.

In 1968, Holly and I traveled to Connecticut to witness a high school friend's marriage. We knew he was gay, and the prospects likely were dim. It was a loud and happy party, but Holly and I ended arguing over a drunk girl's advances to me, and the settlement of the matter ended incredibly in plans to marry several weeks later, I think probably as proof of my dedication to our future together. Holly was in her final year in college, I had just graduated, and students were not allowed to live on campus if married, so we drove to Delaware for a quiet wedding, an elopement.

My brother Roger and best friend Dave were there, and the private chapel business was run by a friendly man; his wife played the piano. We never told our parents but got "engaged" later in the fall. In December my mother and father guessed that the new engagement was tense and unhappy, but I could not explain, even through tears, that we were already married. My mother told me years later that she thought my upset was because Holly was pregnant, which she wasn't. Holly graduated in the spring and we married again, publicly, in her hometown church, with full promise to each other and to God, and with public witness of a hundred people or so.

We struggled with new jobs, graduate study, disagreements about where to live and work. Three years after we married, Holly became ill, and following a stressful move together, an opportunity for me to teach at our old college, we separated. The next year Holly died unexpectedly, complications of her illness. One marriage, two weddings, promises, echoes of "in sickness and in health," and "'til death do us part." I stayed at the college, finished my studies, but traveled a lot, remained unsettled, ending in a research position in Europe, and a chance encounter with Lisbeth, a Danish woman, and new plans, new promises.

In 1976, I traveled several times to Denmark, and Lisbeth came to the States, as I finished my year away from the college. Lisbeth's dream was to live in America, together with her nine-year-old daughter. She had been married once before, and I persisted in describing how we would marry and she then could move to the United States. In 1977 we were married in her hometown outside Copenhagen, just the two of us, in the mayor's office. The marriage contract's promises were hopeful, yet translated into a strange language; likewise the cultural differences between Scandinavia and America, so engaging and enticing, were unhealthy for us both.

The move together to the United States was delayed repeatedly, but Lisbeth finally packed and shipped her belongings and moved. The year back at the college was dismal, work was difficult for Lisbeth to find, her daughter was unhappy, and one of Lisbeth's former male friends stayed in touch, promising a future when she came home to Denmark. Lisbeth made plans to return to Denmark, and with the return to Denmark in sight, things were going better, and she invited me to come with her, if I wanted. Short of a promise, but apparently hopeful. We packed and moved as a family.

In Denmark, things went well; we found a place of our own. She returned to full employment after the previous year of menial jobs in the States; I found work, first teaching English and then in restaurants, and finally teaching Danish to immigrant refugees. Along the way, with wildly conflicting working hours and Lisbeth's daughter moving to a private boarding school, we lost track of the adventure and split up, then divorced. I stayed in Copenhagen for another year, then moved to Jutland, near friends, and finally, age forty, decided to leave the country, go home.

In 1986, I arrived back in the United States and headed for Milwaukee, a fresh start. A friend from college teaching days invited me to stay with him and his wife in an attic apartment in their house. They helped me get readjusted to life in the States, and I traveled in their circle of friends. I landed a substitute teaching job in the public schools and got a full-time position the following year. I also met Angela, lawyer and mother of a six-year-old boy.

Angela came from a prominent Italian family with a thriving restaurant and connections to kin in power. I advanced in my work, became a high school assistant principal within a year, principal two years later. During that same time, Angela and I planned to marry, she for the second time, my third (or fourth, if one counts two with Holly). Angela was Catholic, and I entered into a depressing process of annulment from Lisbeth to be able to marry in Angela's church. Considering earlier promises and plans and the Scandinavian culture, this annulment process focused on an assumed original lack of sincerity of promise or vow on Lisbeth's part, and not my own failure. The process was an insult and a betrayal, but seemed to be required so I could make the new promise. It all felt all wrong, not unlike the second marriage to Holly. But in 1988, Angela and I were married. The priest shared the officiating with my former minister and chaplain father, and I recall the vows and crying silently in my head for God to give me strength to follow through in this commitment, so heavily weighted by families and church and past failures.

Angela and I were in our forties, and we both were moving into new professional arenas; I was advancing in public school administration, and she was transitioning from public school teaching to a high-powered personal injury law practice. Angela could argue any case, and we battled at home about money, of which there was no real lack, about the residency requirement to live within the city limits because of my public job, about her son and the boy's father, about one of Angela's former boyfriends, our mutual long working hours, and more. I got my first high school principal position, and the next year we separated.

Angela did the divorce paperwork, and all was protected by her pre-nuptial agreement that I had gladly signed, having had nothing but an old car and a suitcase when I arrived in town. I moved into a hotel and then bought a house across the street from my high school, and we were divorced as quickly as was possible in the state of Wisconsin. I made plans to move to Virginia, telling all it was to be nearer to my aging parents. I moved the following year.

That was 1992, and I became a high school principal in Page County, Virginia. One September morning, while having coffee in the local café, doing the crossword puzzle, the waitress approached with the coffee pot. After pouring a refill, she asked, simply, "Say, who the hell are you, anyway?" In January, 1994, Betty and I were married in a lawyer's office in Luray. Betty had been married before and had two daughters. The lawyer knew and liked Betty's family and knew that I was a stranger to the county. He was blunt about our need to work at the marriage, and I told him that I had promised to "be there," that I would stay, be faithful, persist, support, just *be there*. For Betty. For the children. For the home. For the future, the years to come.

Twenty years later, I recall those words. In the midst of questions and worries, plans and problems, daily routines and concerns, words of promise, simply that I would be there. And that, in fact, I would.

ℒast ℊtop, 1992

I headed east from Milwaukee and Chicago on the interstate, taking it slowly in the rented van, Aunt Vivian's gray Buick Century on a car trailer behind, two days on the interstate, no rush, then south from Pittsburgh on highways that work their way through West Virginia and into Virginia, the Shenandoah Mountains. On the third day, I had time and plenty of daylight, but stopped in Mount Jackson and called my father and mother to tell them I would be arriving in Page County the next morning. As I expected, they wanted to meet me there. In fact, my father wanted to meet me by the side of the highway, on foot, and drive with me in the truck the last miles to my new home, a doublewide trailer on the west side of the valley, clear view of the eastern sky over the next mountain ridge, about ten miles away.

This was more my father's adventure than mine. In fact, it was no adventure for me: more of a final retreat, a quiet surrender. My father would meet me at the top of the mountain overlooking the Page Valley, and we would drive down and meet my mother, wherever she would have let him out of the car to walk up the road. This day was symbolic for him, something like Moses and Joshua entering the Promised Land, I thought. I had not read carefully enough at that time to know that God had forbidden Moses to enter into Canaan for his sins of disobedience. My father and I drove down the mountain together, into my new life.

My departure from Milwaukee was not as speedy as the flight from Denmark had been a decade earlier, but it was as certain. My mother and father had visited me in Milwaukee, even visited the big high school on the western outskirts of the city where I was principal. A picture that a student took that day shows my parents' age, and I recall thinking, when I first saw them there, how they seemed weakened, worn. My father's chronic cough had worsened; at times, he could not stop wheezing and gagging. Suddenly they were old, and frail. And my father was lonely.

My divorce from Angela was final. I had moved to a hotel downtown and then bought a small house near the high school, and I felt alone and uncertain in the city, which, in a way, was Angela's. And her family's. It was simply time to leave. My father had sent news clippings about some job openings in school divisions in the part of Virginia where they had retired from New York, hoping I might come home. I knew that my father had run out of plans and projects, had no dreams—to travel or write or study or join any groups. And the cough. So, I was on the way to spend my next chapter near to parents, see them into old age and beyond. It was not really my plan, but it was what I told anyone who asked: going to be closer to my parents, who suddenly seemed old and frail, and frightened. My father, at least. I would return to my father.

If I had been asked at that time what the next larger chapter of my life would be about, I imagine I would have described only a year or two, maybe a handful of years, similar to the previous twenty years' record, of too many moves and jobs and relationships and cars and marriages. And plans. But I am not sure that I ever could have predicted the stability, the commitment, and the finality I would experience in Page County. At the time, as I turned the truck and trailer back onto the road at the top of New Market Gap, my father leaning forward in the seat, I never would have guessed the turn toward God I was going to experience in Page County, the deep knowledge that He was riding with me and that He had never been far from my side, even as I ignored or dismissed or defied Him along the way. Maybe not my turn toward God. Maybe His turn toward me. Or maybe He had been watching in the direction I would come, all along.

I had flown east in the spring, to interview for the principal's position in one of the two high schools in the county. The interview was with the school board. They asked many questions, but only one issue stood out: their critical overriding concern over the school's parking lot and student drivers. The board members believed that many kids were leaving the school during the day, skipping school. And they were looking for a fresh answer. One of them suggested a booth at the end of the lot; someone would sit and guard the lot. I thought that maybe he wanted to sit in the booth, a school board member on guard duty. Would they arm the guard? A gun? In Milwaukee, the school squads carried guns.

"What would you do about that, the kids driving away?" Five stares and the superintendent sitting off to one side, silent.

"Tell them they can't. Tell them they can't drive away." Silence. I had walked around the school the evening before with my father, who had picked me up at the airport for the interview the following day. I had noted the gravel parking lot with a couple of cars parked at odd angles. But nowhere was there any broken glass, no tell-tale graffiti or gang signs, no trash, no sirens in the distance. And there was a beautiful, silent view of the mountains. Silent. Blue-gray mountains. This was a really nice place, a jewel in the mountains. Quiet, peaceful, everything in order. Peace.

"Tell them they can't?" Five stares, the superintendent sitting very still.

"Sure. You need to pave the parking lot, line it off, number the parking spaces. Tell them they can't drive away. Not until school's out."

"Parking spaces. Numbers." Silence. The superintendent was turning red. I guessed he wouldn't have a vote in selecting the new principal.

"Assigned spaces. So you know who's missing."

"Know who's missing? And what if they leave?"

"Take away their driving permission." Silence.

"Take away their driving permission? They'll go along with this?" Disbelief.

"To be able to drive? One kid loses his driving privilege for a week, that'll settle it, forever. Or maybe start with an easier rule, give them an easy rule to say yes to, make a habit of going along. Simple expectations. Reasonable. I guarantee they want it." Silence.

"An easier rule. What's an easy rule?"

"No caps in school, maybe." In Milwaukee, I'd told the boys they couldn't wear hats in school, that gentlemen didn't wear hats indoors. Everyone knew it was about the gang colors. "They agree to an easy rule, and that's it." I thought of the peaceful blue mountains and Milwaukee's gangs.

I got the job, they paved the lot, I painted lines and numbered the spaces. I watched the parking lot the same way I watched the halls and the cafeteria and the playing fields. And the mountains. Silent. Deep blue mountains.

It was a beautiful place, filled with deeply respectful children, even when angry, and parents who wanted their kids to thrive and be happy. The view of the mountains was quiet and peaceful. I would learn later on, as the story unfolds, that the mountains, and the children, were daily evidence of God's wonderful creation.

A Cup of Coffee—A Family Story Retold

I believe in connections. Stories and connections. Mr. Talbot, my 12th grade English teacher, liked my story: "A Cup of Coffee." I didn't think Mr. Talbot liked me, thought I was lazy, but he praised my paper and read it out loud to the class. He criticized the obvious ending, that a desperate man's life could be saved by a roadside diner waitress. But he read the paper out loud, the best one turned in. "Good job, Scottie." Proud.

My story was actually true, borrowed from a tale my Aunt Vivian told. Aunt Vivian was a doctor, and our stories were variations on a patient's experience: a depressed man drives toward his lakeside cabin to commit suicide, stops for a cup of coffee in a diner on the way, and connects with a friendly and lonely waitress. He later turns back from his suicide plan to see if there is a chance for a hopeful life with the waitress. My aunt's stories about her patients usually ended happily, part of her treatment, perhaps. Aunt Vivian captured our imagination, unexpected cures for depressed and confused beings. How bad things could be, how fortunate and obvious the rescues. Wonderful stories.

I told Aunt Vivian's story about the man and the waitress and the cup of coffee to friends over the years. I told it often, as an ironic reflection of my own life. Unlucky romances, hopeful yet solitary travels, chance meetings, new beginnings. Loneliness and adventure. Wanderings in the desert. Saving angels.

Aunt Vivian died, having failed to diagnose an aneurism in her own gut. She left her car, a gray Buick, to my mom, who asked if I wanted it. Yes. I lived in Milwaukee and needed a way to travel between an increasingly fragile marriage there and my aging parents in Virginia. The marriage finally collapsed. I loaded a U-Haul, hooked Aunt Vivian's Buick behind, and prepared to set off for Virginia for good. My Milwaukee coffee-drinking pal, Joe Ryan, a rare friend not loyal to my ex-wife's anger, came to say good-bye.

"Safe trip, Scottie." He grinned. "Remember the diner, the waitress. She's there. In Virginia. Waiting. A cup of coffee."

The story. A Cup of Coffee.

"Right. Thanks, Joe."

The trip was longer than usual, breakdowns and fatigue, loneliness. In Virginia, I unpacked in an empty double-wide on a mountainside near Stanley, began preparations for my new job. This was a close community, mountains and hollows, families and histories private, foreign. I found a café in town, a place to go, mostly workers. I settled for coffee, the newspaper and daily crossword puzzle. Not bad, not too lonely in the local crowd.

The Main Street Café in Stanley had no waitress. The owner held court at the cash register, and the cook brought the food. My third visit, newspaper folded to the crossword, I looked up. The cook.

"Say, the others. They're asking. Who the hell are you anyway?" She was tough and smiling. Betty.

"You having coffee today?"

I believe in connections. Stories and connections.

$\mathcal{T}$HE $\mathcal{P}$RODIGAL $\mathcal{S}$ON

I am the prodigal son, ever returning home to regain my life. Sunday afternoon, my father waits on the front porch of the retirement village house in Bridgewater. Most weekends I make the one-hour drive to visit my mom and dad. As I turn the final corner, my father is standing on the porch, looking in the direction I will come. Two, three years, most Sundays.

"Hey, Scottson."

First, we talk about my old pickup truck. Our truck, I guess, as he always finds something to fix on it and usually offers to pay. The truck is freshly painted, but no more trustworthy underneath. Sundays my father waits on the porch. I wonder again if he has been there for hours. Days. Maybe every day. We spend an hour or two, Mother makes some small meal, we talk and eventually walk back to the truck.

My father says, "Be careful. A lot riding on those wheels."

Saturday morning, nursing home. My father sits by the nurse's station. He's in a wheelchair and is wearing a baseball cap, "Gone Fishin'"

163

embroidered on the crown. He seldom wears a hat, hardly a baseball cap, never went fishing. I don't know where he got the cap. My father's life is, was, mind and words. He is ready to go, smiling weakly, not quite sure.

Forgetful, swallowing, choking spell, then four months in assisted living, he goes down fast. His first two days in the medical unit are a nightmare, noise and smells and cries. He cries too. My mother and I sit out of sight in the dining room, watching to see if someone will come, to feed or clean or comfort, anything. No one. I know he is dying.

I tell the nurse I'm taking my father. The nurse says not unless the doctor approves. I tell her he's my dad, and I say I'm taking him, clean him up, feed him. She says I need approval. My father's cap says "Gone Fishin'."

"So we'll take him for the weekend. My wife's a nurse. She's off. We'll bring him back Monday." A lot riding on those wheels. One-way trip, home.

Monday, Dad sits in the room at the back of our house. The small addition was a thought several years ago. He paid. Betty quit her job at the hospital and watches and cares and feeds and cleans, these final seven weeks of my father's life. He sits at the window, points at the birds at the edge of our woods. Or at a splash of sunlight.

"A little piece of heaven," he says.

Seven weeks and silence.

The biblical story about the lost son goes like this; the son comes to his senses and decides he will reclaim his life. *And he arose, and came to his father. But when he was yet a great way off, his father saw him, and had compassion, and ran, and fell on his neck, and kissed him.*

I believe the story is about the father.

$\mathcal{C}$OMING $\mathcal{H}$OME—$\mathcal{W}$RITING "$\mathcal{T}$HE $\mathcal{P}$RODIGAL $\mathcal{S}$ON"

My father retired from Columbia University Teachers College in the early 1980s, and he and my mother moved to Virginia. In the winter of 1991, they visited me in Milwaukee, where I was in my second year as principal of one of the city's big high schools. My parents suddenly looked old and frail, but my father also seemed uncertain and lonely, almost afraid. A student snapped a photo of the three of us on the front steps of the school, and the image guided my unexpected and fresh plans to pack up and head homeward.

My father's tension and unease and age during that Milwaukee visit gave birth to complex feelings of impending loss and indebtedness, responsibility, and fear that I had not experienced before. I told anyone who asked that I was going home to be near my aging parents, but it was about my father. And it was about me.

In actuality, I was worn out from one more failed marriage, one more adventure come to naught, another brief chapter in a life woven of dreams and successes, detours and disappointments, projects and divestments, and incessant travel. My brilliant father had done the same, until a faithful dean rehired him for a third and threatened last time. He remained at Columbia for more than twenty years, until his retirement.

I was to do the same thing, leaving solid success after only two years at Vincent High School in Milwaukee and investing sixteen years until my own retirement as a high school principal in the Shenandoah Valley, only an hour from my parents. I visited them often; then weekly, on Sundays, after my father became ill.

The biblical account of the prodigal son places the young man at the center of the story. While the father is the eternal benefactor of all rewards, the son is the ultimate beneficiary of grace. But the father waits and watches steadfastly and sees the son when he is yet a long way off. The father weeps for joy. Despite his wealth and limitless understanding, he had no assurance that the son would return to his senses, or to his home, or to his true inheritance. Hence the father's joy at the son's homecoming.

In my father's and my case, I can only guess how much my father longed for even the brief moments of a son's companionship and love during his final years. I know that in the end, he would have not been comforted without the support and protection of son and nurse daughter-in-law. But even more important for me, I believe that after a lifetime of wandering and waste, I chose to go to my father, to reclaim my life by giving him the only thing he could not create for himself. And most important of all, on Sunday afternoons, he was always waiting. And watching. Watching in the direction I would come.

FINAL CALL. FINAL LETTER

You called late one evening, and you were drunk. That was the last time we spoke, and I think you were calling because you were angry about my not being in touch with Birgitte. She was my pride and joy stepdaughter, but she embarrassed everyone when she visited in Milwaukee and then left without a good-bye. Perhaps I was just too disappointed. But you called, drunk, and lied to Betty about who you were, tried to give me an address and e-mail to contact you later on. I never tried, never took down the information, never even thought of trying.

Not to say that drifting and then ripping apart weren't the most awful days of my life. Your culture and your ways were dangerous and unkind. Do you remember driving in Jutland, at the very first part of our relationship, and when the car broke down you flirted and exchanged information with the stranger behind the Alfa Romeo service desk? Do you remember that we stopped at a hotel north of Copenhagen to retrieve a bracelet or a watch you had left in a room, the tall singer Michael who took you on that side trip? And do you remember how we met, your job was to do the tickets and hotels, but the brewery owner wanted more? There was probably no way to avoid the poison that was resident in our hearts from the beginning, and I guess I just believed that it was part of the Danish way of life.

I regret going to cooking school in London after baby Mymla died. You may not have needed me with you, but it was the beginning of the end, to disappear for months, just at that time. I regret now that I took jobs that kept me away for nights and weekends, investing my all in a new Danish working life. I am sorry I fell so easily for what I thought was the Danish way, easy adventures, stay out, no excuses, travels alone, away from each other. I regret now that I did not beg us to retrieve the better days, instead demanding a final decision just at a time when there was no information in our favor.

And then, suddenly, it was over, and despite the sadness, the sorrow, the loss, it was just over, and you had moved on.

I remember that you tried to set me up with another Lisbeth, that you invited me to cater your wedding to your new guy, Hasse. I remember you suggested that I move to Ribe and assume the dad's role in your dead uncle's home. And some agreed with you, that it was a good idea. Then it was time to go, time to cut the ties, and suddenly it is twenty or thirty years later. This is my final letter.

TRAPPED

Our two turkey houses are shorter than most, four hundred forty feet, but wider, seventy feet. The starter ends are at the front of each house for the little birds, with a partition and sliding door separating starter ends from the grow-out ends. The grow-out is more than twice the length of the starter end. I walk through the two starter ends and then come outside and head toward the small door on the side wall, where I can go into one of the grow-outs.

With only two houses, it's not too much to check each morning, mostly walking, picking up dead or sick birds for the composter, checking for any equipment malfunctions, water leaks, feed spills. Pretty much everything is automated—feed, water, medication, heat, ventilation, and light, and I can finish in an hour or two before going to work at the high school. I repeat this twice-daily check in the late evening, before going to bed, and I save the heavy work for the weekends, cleaning out, repairs, spreading used litter or storing it in the litter shed. Seven days a week.

We have just under fifty thousand turkeys, about twelve thousand five hundred in each of the four sections, when all sections are populated. The big birds, about thirteen weeks old, will go away in a week or so, and then I'll sift the worst litter in the grow-out, top-dress with saved starter litter, and move the little birds up through the big inside doors, a nerve-wracking process, herding skittish and excited five-week-old birds through the opening, at the same time trying to keep them from rushing back through the door as we go back for more. The whole process is repeated four or five times each year, never ending, more than a hundred twenty-five thousand birds a year. We like our turkeys, talk to them, and try to make things as fresh and comfortable as possible.

The sun is just coming up, and it will be a warm day. I can hear the clanking of the feed auger at the far end of the houses, drawing feed from the two twenty-foot steel tanks on each side of the grow-outs. The starter units have single, smaller tanks one-third of the way along the drive lane separating the two houses. There is a clunk-clunk sound from a feed auger, sounding more metal-on-metal than usual, sounds like an empty auger, perhaps a tank is empty or feed clogged somewhere, not dropping down into the feed line auger. I squint to see down the three hundred feet and see there's a feed spill, a big one, outside under the tanks. I see feed out on the cement pad under both tanks on one side of the gravel lane, the feed flowing out over the grass and onto the driveway, not a small spill, perhaps a ton, maybe more.

I run to the end of the house, tank and auger clanking an urgent tune, open the service door on the end of the house and go in, eyes adjusting to the dim grow-out. The clanking is coming from the inside feeders as well, as they are empty and no feed is getting to the feed lines or pans. The birds are noisy, confused, hungry. I shut off the feed tank motors and then walk back through the house to shut off the feed lines.

It's a big mess, and I'll have to try to fix the feeding quickly, but won't be able to clean up the spill outside until after work at school, the afternoon at the earliest.

Outside, I clear away some of the feed from under the tanks, kicking it away with my boot, and see that the feed has spilled from both tanks. I quickly find that the feed line auger inspection plates at the bottom of both tanks are missing, and that feed has been spreading across the pad and ground instead of going into the houses to the feed lines and pans. Both tanks. Vandalism is my first thought. Too much of a coincidence for both inspection plates to be off. And where are they? How can I cover the openings?

I jog back to the generator building and grab some feed sacks and a shovel to clear feed away. We've had no vandalism, other than a few .22 rounds through the siding, accidental perhaps. Some of the neighbors have been upset with us from the start of construction, the commercial poultry operation spoiling their view of the mountains, and one of two rights-of-way across our property blocked to keep traffic and potential for disease as far from the birds as possible. But there are three other poultry houses, chickens, a thousand feet further down the slope, so we've never taken the complaint to heart; poultry houses everywhere in the county. But now, with this, vandalism, so very hard to manage or stop.

I find one of the auger inspection plates directly under one tank's auger, buried under a foot or two of feed I've cleared away. At least the vandals didn't take it or throw it in the woods. I find the other inspection plate directly under the second tank, so at least I will be able to cover the openings and start the feeding up again, clean up the huge feed spill later. Then I notice the blood on the second auger plate and on the bottom of the tanks. Blood in the feed, too. And when I shovel the bloody feed away, blood on the ground. And tracks. Animal tracks, larger than a dog's paw.

An animal. Not likely a dog after turkey feed anyway, and on the edge of the National Forest, maybe a bear. Relief it wasn't a neighbor's teen, or a neighbor himself. But a bear. What do you do about a bear?

I walk to the workroom and call the poultry company's service line for advice: what to do? Does this ever happen, or often? Could it be a bear? The answer is quick and sure. Yes, it's probably a bear, and lucky it didn't destroy the plastic boot at the bottom of the tanks or the feed line. Or that it didn't hang around, angry about a bloody paw. Call the trapper, he'll work with you. A trapper? Trap the bear? Yes, he will trap the bear and take it away. I dial the number the serviceman gives me, and the Game and Inland Fisheries bear trapper answers. A bear trapper.

We are in luck, and he can come in the afternoon. He tells me it's important because the bear will be back, having found a source of food, unless he's hurt badly. The blood might not be from his paw, but from his muzzle or tongue, lapping at feed when the auger clicked on. It's the fish meal in the turkey feed. He can smell it a mile away, and hungry enough to approach a steel tank and machinery. Fish meal. Like salmon in a Northwest rapids, a bear scooping fish out of the river. A bear and a feed tank, an auger clanking like silver river waves breaking over the rapids.

The trapper arrives on time, a forest-green pickup truck with a large steel culvert on the back, and a winch to unload it. The culvert is a heavy mesh steel cage with legs and a door and latch system, a pretty obvious trap. I would think it unlikely any wild animal would venture into that contraption, but the trapper assures me his bait, scraps from Virginia hams, will do the trick. He unloads the trap and I help him heave and shove it into place in the grass beside one of the tanks. I ask if maybe the bear was just passing through. Not likely, and now he knows there's food. So where is the bear? The trapper points up the hill, the mountainside a mile away, rock outcroppings and gravel slides. Probably up there, watching us. Or else down behind the shed, he says, pointing at the composter building fifty feet away. Watching. Or sleeping. But he'll be back. Tonight, or tomorrow morning.

The trapper hangs the ham trimmings on the latch mechanism's hook in the far end of the cage and props the heavy door up, setting the release system and the bars that lock the door in place when it falls. He tells me to call when the bear is in the trap, or if it trips the door before going in, or if a dog or other animal trips the door. If the bear trips it from the outside, he will either run away or stay and cause more damage to the feed tanks.

The next morning, it's quiet at the turkey houses. I drive the two hundred yards to the farm early, anxious to see if the bear has come back. I can hear one of the feed augers, the usual ticking sound. And I can already see that the door on the trap is closed, latched. I walk down between the turkey houses, wondering if the door is locked securely. In the dusky dawn light, I can see a large, dark shape inside the trap. Very large. Quiet. A black bear, I believe, maybe two or three hundred pounds. I can hear it snuffling. But quietly, almost gently. And still.

The trapper answers on the first ring and says he'll be out directly. I ask if he will destroy the bear. No, of course not. Take it back to the park? He laughs out loud, tells me a minimum of forty, maybe fifty miles are needed to put between this bear and our farm. Of course, he may find another feed tank between that place and here. When the trapper arrives, he is impressed. The bear is over five hundred pounds, he thinks. He winches the trap and bear up ramps onto the pickup truck. The bear remains quiet, shifting weight as the trap slides up the ramps, onto the truck, but quiet. The trapper and I talk a bit, but he has a long drive and a schedule to meet and leaves shortly.

It's still early, plenty of time to walk through and check the birds. For the dead and the sick. One of the augers clicks on, and feed grinds through the tubes. Fifty thousand birds, eating, waiting. Fifteen weeks. Trapped.

$\mathcal{O}$ NE $\mathcal{C}$ LEAR $\mathcal{M}$ EMORY, 2008

This exercise is so easy, so incredibly clear, a moment that I relive again and again. It took place only five years ago, but reminds me so often of salvation, relief, rescue from humiliation, remarkable good fortune, coincidence, luck, and kindness of folks who didn't notice. You expect, of course, something about a miraculous healing, a heavenly revelation, sexual escapade, birth of a child or grandchild. No. Nothing quite so elementary or extraordinary; this was very commonplace.

We drove in two school buses from Page County to Washington, DC: one hundred seniors on a government class trip, weeks before graduation from high school. I was the principal, retiring that year, and my daughter Sheena was along on the trip, graduating that June herself. We drove in two buses, and I sat at the front of the second bus. The driver was an old bus driver colleague, Elva, and Ginny Brown sat across from me, my senior government teacher. The students on our bus sat several rows behind us, and then .all the way to the rear of the bus. We were making good time and nearing Washington when we passed a rest stop. Elva asked if we had any need to stop. I thought about it and said no, we had only been driving for an hour or so, and we'd be in DC within twenty minutes.

No sooner had we passed the rest stop than I began to notice a faint need to pee. The thought shocked me slightly, but we would be in DC within twenty or thirty minutes, and that would be no problem. Except that I now had the matter on my mind, and the traffic was gathering, more congested and slowing somewhat. The highway began to widen to three and four and five lanes, and access was only to other highways. There were no side streets, no gas stations, no exits. But we had time enough. Until we began to slow, then to stop and go. Then stop. I began to feel a growing urge, a need to find a bathroom. The bus was standard yellow school bus and had no restroom.

You may find this less than compelling as a true "One Clear Memory," but I was the principal, the father, the protector, the old man. I began to wonder about relieving myself by the side of the road, asking them to just stop, or turn down another side highway in hopes that a fresh super-highway might have an exit to a gas station. I wondered what it might be like to pee in my pants so early in the day, fifty miles from home, a hundred kids witness. Or YouTube footage of the principal behind the bus, in traffic, peeing in a lineup of stopped cars, horns honking. The surrounding was simply concrete and asphalt, strangers, and school children for whom I had the ultimate responsibility. And one hundred potential reports to the county when they arrived home, plenty of room for exaggeration.

The traffic grew heavier and heavier, though I could see we were approaching the bridges and entryways to the city, perhaps a solution, but my insides were nearing an uproar of frantic need. Calm thoughts, displaced by pangs and twinges. On a bridge coming into the city. Certainly someplace to stop in town. No, just the opposite.

Washington traffic was even tighter, and every building seemed to be a federal agency or museum, closed at this early hour, gray office structures, pedestrians and police everywhere. Center of the nation gearing up for a busy day, crowds walking and watching everywhere. Parks and open spaces, and I was beyond panic; I was just going to pee, and there was no other way.

We stopped at one more red light in heavy traffic, police, and pedestrians everywhere.

"Open the door, Elva! I'll meet you at the next light!"

Crowds, parting around a cement blockhouse on the corner of the parkway. I was sure the kids were wondering too, and I went around the far side of the tiny building. Two shrubs eight feet tall guarded an old, locked doorway, just visible past the greenery. I pushed through, wedged myself further in between shrubs and building, and somehow zipped and grabbed and aimed without making any mistakes. I did not care if I got arrested, did not care if the kids knew what I was about, as they couldn't see, and I was in utter, primal relief. Period. I was saved, I was delivered. Forgiven. I finished, ready to go in half a minute. I backed out of the bushes, no one in the city even noticed, and when I came around the corner of the building, the buses were still there, waiting.

"What's up, Doc?" asked Elva.

"Just checking things out. We're OK."

I was the principal. And I was fine. The light turned green, and we rolled forward into a new day. For weeks I caught myself laughing out loud.

"Thank you, Jesus! Thank you for saving my life!" The salvation was real, tangible, and the memory, however mundane, truly one that I visit more often than any other, reliving panic, recalling how the way opened, and giving thanks to God for deliverance. I remember it, again, like it was yesterday.

$\mathcal{N}$O $\mathcal{W}$HINING: $\mathcal{H}$EART OF $\mathcal{D}$ARKNESS

Heart of Darkness was my favorite book in high school, and maybe of all time. I remember its mystery, its danger, and the final desperate words spoken by Kurtz. I remember his name, and Marlow's. The captain. Death. Africa. Ivory. I knew it well. I carried the story—no, my love of the book, all my adult life; always named it when asked about my favorite book. *Heart of Darkness*, Conrad. Kurtz and Marlow. My favorite book. Until I read it, or heard it on a CD. And I am ashamed to take the blame that Goldberg applies to the casual reader without purpose and without determination or investment.

Without courage. *Heart of Darkness*. I bought the CD, thinking it would be nice to revisit my favorite book. When I heard the story, riding to work at the college in the fall of 2009, I recognized a fragment or two at the beginning of the story, but began to realize there was much I had forgotten. Forgotten, or not read at all, or at least never finished. The book was rich and troubled and ironic and ended with a tragic and false consolation message to a grieving woman, Kurtz's last words. I had never read the book, just dabbled in emotion and some disjointed thoughts, turned a few pages. My favorite book in high school.

SONGS

I listen to music in the car. The iPod is pure luxury. It plays through the car's audio system, and if there's a phone call coming in, the music cuts out and I can talk. I sing along, mostly bass line or harmony, but the most lonesome lines and soaring emotion can take me anywhere in the scale, even falsetto. But who's listening?

My favorite songs…maybe "A Remark You Made," Weather Report, from the 1970s. Jaco Pastorius's bass guitar solos are treasures. I heard that he was dead, but how could that be? His "Remark" is pure heaven, a wistful memory of when and where I first heard it, Denmark, bohemian times before the squalls.

I have many such songs. Santana's "Europa (Earth's Cry Heaven's Smile)," also 70s, and of course Santana always degenerates his story line into frantic babble too loud for the plaintive first cry. I first heard the song in a bar on the lakefront in Luzern, in September 1977. Jukebox, and I played it over and over. It captured my loneliness and my hunger and has remained my favorite.

Last choice, Santo & Johnny, "Sleep Walk," 50s guitar instrumental, and playing just when I first fell in love. Northfield, rock and roll country high school, and I was in junior high. Real love, real time, and both the emotion and the tune live on. Amazingly, just yesterday, I found another picture of the girl, thirteen years old. Taken in 1959. And iTunes brings me "Sleep Walk." In the car, Interstate 81 North, to work. Heaven.

$\mathcal{O}$ B S E S S I O N

It's all about food, trucks, women, quiet, books, radios, exotic travel, arriving home, praise, words, and more. Food is hidden, trucks and women just to look at, longing for comfort and quiet. Capture plans and thoughts in books on the shelf, admiration for the places I've been. Yes, I can too. Speak Danish and German, a little Italian and Spanish and French to get by, play the piano, and strum the guitar. All accumulated, but not practiced. I can gather them all in, line them up, but don't use them, hardly practice, never quite competent. Except the Danish, but where can you speak Danish?

The food is fat, rich, spiced, salty. But fat, and therefore hidden. Quick cleanup and eat alone. None is for sharing. Stolen, mine. All mine.

Toys and objects from a hundred places, friends. A thousand. I've been there. I knew him. I ran that race, won sometimes. Let me tell you. Words. History. Ribbons. Mother watched. Northfield and Westtown.

COFFEE

I am drinking my first cup of coffee. It is my time, all else stops, and it's comfort to me. I drink it sweet and cream. I prefer strong coffee, as we served it in Bøf & Ost and Peder Oxe, the restaurants on Gråbrødretorvet. Push-down carafes, large amounts of coarsely ground coffee mixed with boiling water, allowed to steep, the strainer-plunger pressed down, the whole pot taken to the table. Strong coffee, and then a chance to enjoy a moment. So it's not the taste, not the aroma, not the caffeine, but the addictive moment.

When I moved to Jutland and lived alone, coffee was my companion. I went to bed late at night, no, early in the morning, and already wondering about my first cup of coffee in the morning. The addiction for coffee matched the demand my mind and body placed for cigarettes, particularly the strong European brands, another signal of time to myself, a moment, a taste, and a comfort.

Coffee and cigarettes were my companions. I've since left cigarettes behind, their use leading to physical pain in my chest. But coffee is still a constant companion and a close friend. If I turn my back on coffee for a day, a thundering headache reminds me, and it takes time to make amends.

This cup of coffee, today, is like the best of all the others; I am on the porch, alone. Thoughts and memories and a rich and addictive sense of the past, the moments, and the day to come.

SITTING MEDITATION

This life I have been living, some days barely living. I have to have an excuse to take ten minutes, even steal the minutes for reading the Bible or breathing deep, wondering if anyone is going to call with a need or something forgotten: quick—bring some things to the car. Or unload the groceries. This is the life I've been living, and in the quietest moments wondering if I'm flying on great business or dying. A tightness across the chest, wonder what I've forgotten. Clothes in the dryer, dishes by the sink or left at the table, I'll get them, hurry up, as time's getting late. Seems like everyone's free and easy and talking and laughing, and why am I worried about it? Get up at 5 a.m. and late going out the door at 7:30. Steal a side trip to 7-11 for a cup of coffee, planning out the day as I go to bed. I fall asleep before I notice that I'm in bed and wake up at 4:00, dull throb and revolving thoughts about things undone or not to solve. I gather complaints and wants and needs and steal an hour Saturday morning in the car, *Click and Clack* and *Wait, Wait, Don't Tell Me*. What kind of life is this, the habit of getting up, making tea and coffee, pour one, leave it on the bathroom counter, get up Betty, read four chapters in the Bible, make lunch and eat, don't forget the vitamins, feed the dog, seed the birds, water the planters, wake the child, pour cereal, glass of water, shower, dress, write a check for the cafeteria at school, rush to the car, back out slow, and breathe deep, go. 7:28, I'm OK; a minute later,

I'll get behind the special ed bus in New Market, stop and go to Mount Jackson. Oh my, and what's in the day coming? Have I forgotten, and is this what I can do, or can I pay the bills, or what about insurance? Briefcase in the back seat, I hope, pull it over, look for the calendar and checkbook, be sure I have what I need. This is my life, in ten minutes, and it's not getting better, but was supposed to be, each day, better.

ᏟHE ᏒOAD TO ᎬMMAUS

*But their eyes were holden, that they should
not know him.*

LUKE 24:16 KJV

It's seven miles from Allentown to Emmaus, Pennsylvania. And just like
in the biblical account, a person could walk the distance, with a friend
perhaps, and talk over the events of the day, or questions about the past
and future, troubles, regrets, plans, anything. I never walked the road to
Emmaus, but drove often, over the years, to visit with my second father,
and for quite a time my father of choice, Jack MacConnell. And his wife,
Helene.

Jack MacConnell's friendship, his presence and influence in my life,
frame the early years of my adult life, my undergraduate education at
Muhlenberg College, late 1960s, where he was one of my professors, my
marriage to Holly, my first teaching jobs in New Jersey schools, graduate
study, and then the years I worked with him in the education department at Muhlenberg, the years of travel away from the States and back,
marriages to Lisbeth, Angela, and Betty, his retirement to what he and
Helene called "the mountain" in Potter County, and finally, his bedside
in a Harrisburg hospital, and his death. Almost thirty years, in all.

My own father was also a college professor, but Jack was everything else my father was not. Jack drove motorcycles, raced a championship Lotus sports car in the Pennsylvania hill climb circuit, hunted deer and squirrel in the mountains, and claimed he was half-blood Sioux. Jack had been an air force turret gunner during the Second World War, crash-landed in the North African desert, sustained sun damage to his eyes and was blind in one. The reason he competed in hill climb racing, he claimed: no other cars or drivers to endanger. Jack never said whether the racing officials knew he was blind in the one eye. I saw his trophies but never got a chance to watch him race.

When Jack called me to work at Muhlenberg, in 1970, I was surprised, and in the end, glad. And fortunate. He told me it required that I go beyond the master's degree I was working on at Columbia for a teacher's pay raise and enter a doctoral program, something I never would have done otherwise, working full-time in a New Jersey intermediate school. I do not believe that I actually returned to Muhlenberg to teach. Within a year following my return to Allentown, I had bought mountain land in Potter County, built a small cabin, bought a motorcycle and then another, bigger one, drove a four-wheel-drive truck much like Jack's, purchased CB radios, hunting knives, and several guns. Jack and I went deer hunting only once, but I never even saw a deer, satisfied just to take part. With my chosen dad.

Jack and Helene liked my wife, Holly. She had been one of his students, too. He helped find a teaching job for her in Allentown when we finally planned our return, and never said a word when she and I parted ways just before school started; neither when she died the following year. He never commented directly on matters of my choices, travels, or my wilder plans, including leaving Muhlenberg for study in Switzerland and then a permanent move to Denmark. He asked only brief and quiet questions, particularly if integrity and consistency were involved; perhaps the Native American in Jack. I wonder if things would have been different if he had openly warned, or cautioned, or advised as my life unfolded and unraveled during those years.

So I credit Jack MacConnell with my first college teaching job at age twenty-six, too young; my doctoral degree a year later, luckily finished;

and for supporting quietly my application for faculty study in Switzerland after four years at Muhlenberg. He had struggled with his own dissertation for years and years, doing original translations of German histories of charity schools in Colonial America. My entire doctoral study took only two-and-a-half years, including dissertation, while teaching school and then college full time, with only a semester off following Holly's death. My dissertation, in contrast to Jack's, was a quick and light treatise on how novels illuminate so much of what we do in schools. But most important was his presence, as father, over all those years, quietly supportive, nodding, smiling, tamping his pipe, as I visited and told what I had done, where I had been, how it all had happened, and what was next. As I best recall, Jack seldom asked for reasons.

When Helene called to tell that Jack's cancer had taken a serious, bad turn, I went to visit him in the hospital in Pennsylvania. Jack had been warned to quit smoking, but Helene knew that he had hidden his pipe in the equipment shed, and that walks with the dog usually ended up in the shed. I drove to Harrisburg on a Sunday afternoon, and I had some things I was determined to share with Jack, if I could get up the courage to share them. Despite his Sioux blood, he never expressed any thoughts on spiritual matters. In fact, Jack was openly skeptical and suspicious of anything related to religion, nearly scornful when it came to churches. But I felt I owed Jack a message about something I had discovered, learned, knew, and wondered where I could even begin.

Jack struggled with the morphine pump and with catching his breath. He was pleased to see me, but uncomfortable, and I think even embarrassed with his situation, his helplessness, his discomfort. We sat quietly, he asked a question or two about Betty and the one daughter he had met, and we shared some news about Muhlenberg people we remembered. Helene came and went, in and out of the room, sensing the coming loss, I guessed. It was a sad moment and contradicted everything Jack meant to me, his strength and humor, his zest for life, his command of so many things that would excite and encourage any father's son. Any dad's boy.

After an hour or so, I left, drove home, helpless. I since have been able to tell some of the things I learned and experienced during those years, 1965 to 1995, though I struggle still with telling anyone what I wanted to tell Jack that day, what I wanted Jack to know. What I knew and had planned to say. Or perhaps that day I still wasn't quite sure.

$\mathcal{B}$ R O K E N

I have been broken once or twice before, maybe three, and only for a time, with a clear way forward building. I am not broken, but I am breaking again, and not in much control of it, and the breaking grows. I awaken in the morning with dread and regret. I am filled with a sense that I have wasted so many opportunities and betrayed so much trust and support, and that it has added up to nothing very significant. It takes an hour or two to regain the day, see the future, make plans, plant my feet on a worthwhile view of what I am about.

At twenty-seven, in the car, driving to New York for classes, the only private place I had, I cried out for help in hopeless loss and misery, Holly dead and no plan or reason. At forty, in Denmark, I knew that I was at a dead end, and that I faced certain destruction if I stayed. So I sold out, packed, and moved. But today, each day more intense, the dreadful sense of worthlessness and meaningless end to it all.

I am fortunate to have the day's business to attend to, enough pull and need and urgency to keep me from breaking, but the take-tens and the memoirs, and the thoughts and the imaginings on paper, add up to a breaking dream that all was worthwhile. The adventures and the travels and the projects and the lovers and the times and the places. My belief that it is a story worth telling and retelling is breaking.

$\mathcal{A}$CHE

I have an ache in my chest, right in the middle, solar plexus or heart or lungs, I don't know. It is most present first thing in the morning, a reminder that all is not right, not settled or resolved, a stress point. It takes an hour or two to process the concern and begin the day with solid anticipation. The tightness in my chest is stress, worry, anxious thoughts, questions too complex to answer or just repeated over and over. I worry that the ache represents a breakdown in confidence that things will work out. The ache is also related to the pace of decision and communication, the immediacy of response, the demand to arrive at reasonable and workable conclusions within moments and with consensus. Worries become collective gatherings, and my chest filters them out, distills discontent and consolidates it, keeps it, regards it.

The e-mail at work is the worst, driving worry directly to my chest. A message to "LFCC Everyone," anger about a perceived threat, dismay and disappointment. Someone responds *Reply All*, ensuring collective outrage, collective disbelief, and agreement among an appointed most against the perceived few. My body responds with tension, a twisting of capillaries and nerve endings, junction in my chest, next to my heart, over the lungs, and I am aware of short breaths, halting, held too long.

Breathe deep, count to five, exhale, in through the nose, out through the mouth, tongue on roof of the mouth. Eyes closed, picture the resolution, visualize the future, the outcome. A moment on the problem, a deep breath, and hold on the perfect solution. I notice that the ache is gone.

$\mathcal{T}$ H E $\mathcal{P}$ U L L

I cannot single out the pull of any particular woman. At a distance of place and time, the pressure is equal: here and there, this one and that. Each encounter held its promise. Each wonder contained a dream, fresh birth and redemption, salvation. I remember a woman in a donut shop in Ohio. Tom and I were driving west, vacation. The woman smiled and perhaps invited me to share a moment. Smile, and good-bye. Then driving, wondering if I couldn't just return and stop traveling, live in this small town and resign the journey.

Or a hospital aide, standard backrub and kind words the night before a small operation. The curtain was drawn, and it was quiet and cool. She had a limp, like the young polio kids I remembered. She asked gently what I would do for the summer vacation. "My wife and I are going to visit her folks in Philly." The moment was broken, and she left. I am pulled to the possibility of that brief exchange. I wonder what if; I wonder where she is.

I remember neighbor girl Marianne. She and I were innocent ages twelve and thirteen when our family moved to Minnesota; and Brigid in Minnesota, who moved to California the same time we returned east, age fourteen. Uprooted, on the road, disappointed, distracted, detoured. Pulled by so many connections, remaining possibility. I wonder. What if.

$\mathcal{F}$LASHBACK - $\mathcal{R}$EVISITED

I remember it all so clearly, once I turn the pages back. So often, it's shame or uneasiness or regret or just something lost. Last night I turned back a page, visiting the street where I had worked for three years, the apartment complex where I had lived. They both looked shabby, run-down, cold, and colorless. It was a view from Google Earth, and suddenly I did not want to visit or flee from today into yesterday. And I recall so many other times when an actual visit to the past resulted not in joyous rediscovery, but in impatience and a desire to move on.

My memories are less fond than sad. I regret the passing of years, and my own eventual passing from the scene. I consider my child Bianca's impatience with me and my nervous insistence on her behavior. She will remember how uncomfortable it was to be in our house, how demanding, and will not know the sentimental treasures I hold of my earlier years, which were, at the time, so full of pain and impatience, like hers.

I need to draw my years together, and to a close, so that I can enjoy a period of accepting rest, of joy in being alive, of easy breathing without distraction or demand. I need to bring things to a conclusion and to a corporate whole. Then I believe I can rest without worry or regret or aspiration or fear. To reach this point, I will write until nothing more flows, until all the stories have been told, all the grievances aired.

$\mathscr{P}$LACE—$\mathscr{A}$LDER $\mathscr{L}$AKE

Alder Lake is on the Gunflint Trail, northern Minnesota, perhaps fifty miles west of Grand Marais on Lake Superior. Alder Lake was in a chain of lakes we canoed in the summer of 1959 or 1960. I was fourteen and romantic about such places. Granite rock sliding down to iron water, cutting cold, quiet and solitary. No one lived here, but I fancied the solitude, maybe even during the winter months. How close this was to heaven, a picture of peace and clarity and oneness. The canoe trip continued on, lakes connected by handy portage trails, campsites, and maps. The evenings were ceremonies of preparation, fire, food, soft talk, and sleep to the sounds of paradise. Rain, wind in pine trees, unknown sounds, movement in the dark, and sleep.

Dave, my high school roommate, often talked of a winter excursion to Alder Lake, how beautiful it must have been and how remote and mystical it would be in the chilling winter. My romantic teenage thought was always that Lake Alder would be the place to go to live the final months of a life well lived, and to have my ashes scattered. My wish. Eagle in the treetop. Call. Sail.

WORDS AND LONELINESS - REVISITED

From my father I learned that words captured ideas, and that one could formulate a future working at one's desk with pen and paper. My father wrote at his desk in the study. He was chaplain at Carleton in our youngest years, and he read his sermons to us at the dinner table, turning off the classical music station before clearing his throat and reading. Fifteen or twenty minutes at the most, and my brother Roger and I didn't understand much of what he was saying, but the logic and the clarity were obvious. He was convincing, we were sure, ideas and encouragements and facts and beliefs crafted into a predictable shell.

What I learned was very different from what my brother learned. I sat and took it in, a five-year-old understanding the weight of words, and my brother, six years old, likely began to make ultimate plans for escape, for refusal, for rebellion. The tension in the dining room was as tight as the silence surrounding the speech. We sat, waited impatiently for the end of the exercise. Release came shortly, we were excused from the table, and Roger left to pursue his own interests while I ran to play, to ride, to draw, to find friends. But I am sure my soul heard the words, the construction, the flow of ideas and arguments, the logic, the surety, the possibility.

But the other thing I learned from my father was loneliness and isolation and rootlessness. He was restless, moving from job to job, from study to study, traveling extensively as if to find something, and ended in a quiet and lonely retirement. I am sure that my father was deeply afraid of death, and that he never rested comfortably. My father had many colleagues, but no real friends. I know that I never experienced him in any setting with other persons, in storytelling, light entertainment, tender sharing, enjoying food, having confidently quiet moments. Never. So, from my father, I have gained the surety of words and ideas, and the transience of existence.

$\mathcal{F}$ATHER'S $\mathcal{L}$AST $\mathcal{L}$ECTURE

I did not attend Father's final lecture. It took place in the dining room on the assisted living floor at the nursing home, during lunch. Thirty, perhaps forty persons were there, eating and talking. It was springtime, in the weeks prior to Father's move to the medical department, away from Mother, out of sight. I did not attend the final lecture; nor do I know if mother was with him when he rose to speak, or how much attention she paid if she was there, but the nurses reported it to us.

They said father stood up at the table, food untouched. He looked around, waited for a bit, and then began to prepare his thoughts out loud, supplying what they reported were bits and pieces of thought on a subject that was complex and sounded quite important, but which was entirely unclear. He spoke for several minutes, all the time surveying his audience, clearing his throat. I was not there, but I can hear his voice.

Father used big words and smiled as he made his point. He used conditional and parenthetical, paraphrase and background support, comments and asides. Single words containing complicated threads of meaning and intent. He listed the expected objections to his argument, counters to his thesis, and I am sure he asked the audience to interrupt if anyone had a question or concern.

I can see him standing at his table, surveying the people in the room, most eating and ignoring his presentation. Perhaps, just for a moment, he realized that the thoughts were not lining up right, that what he knew to be true was not playing out smoothly, much as in the times he stepped forward into the elevator with us when we gathered ourselves to leave after a visit. I am sure he knew his circumstance, at least in fleeting moments.

I did not attend Father's last lecture. Even so, I know in my heart that his intent was not to impress, but to gather together the words that would capture the essence, the meaning, of something that had escaped him all the days of his life.

FIGHTING MOM

The fights were always the same, from the earliest time I can remember my mother's guidance until the weeks before she died at age ninety-five. She was righteous and confident. She was careful and correct. Her take on things was the only acceptable one, and she didn't always give her reasons for her choice. The fights were typically over the most petty and mundane issues of safety and decorum. Things like sunburn and saying thank you, or simply standing up straight. Or zipping up a coat.

The last time my mother and I fought was perhaps the worst, because it was a mother-and-child issue, and I was nearly sixty years old. I was in the pool, our backyard above-ground small version of luxury. After a tedious week's work at the high school, I lay on a plastic float and drifted lazily in circles, gathering in late-afternoon sunrays through the trees, thinking about the birds and the next day's chores and nothing much else in particular. Mother lived in a small addition at the back of the house, and she had a door from her room out onto the narrow porch and wheelchair ramp next to the pool. She levered the screen door open and wobbled out on her cane and stood for a few minutes at the railing. She did not ask anything about my day or week but simply prodded me, "Scottie, don't you think it's time to get out of the pool?"

"No, Ma, I just got in and it's nice and quiet and plenty of time until supper."

"I think it's time you got out of the pool."

"Ma…" I had always called her Mother until my father died, five years previous. Dad had had a range of names: Father, or my brother called him Phil; and we nicknamed him Dean when he worked in that capacity at the college. He became Dad only when he was on his last legs, wasting away and slipping into forgetfulness. When he became Dad, Mother became Ma. Not quite disrespectful, but certainly so when we fought. Or when she fought, as I never began an argument with a parent.

"Ma-a…!" The evening was ruined, as she wouldn't leave the porch.

"Ma, I'm sixty years old!"

"Ma, I'll know when it's been long enough."

"Ma!" She stood her ground, cane angling back and forth and glaring, no way to convince her otherwise.

I do not know who won the last battle, though she died that year. I don't know if she saw a five-year-old in the sharp sun, or a child in the water too soon after lunch, or strangers lurking in an imaginary poolside park. I'll never know, but I remember so clearly how the afternoon was ruined, and even when she finally retreated to her room, the bitterness of my defiance lingered too long. I remained on the water but had lost the fight. Clearly.

$\mathscr{L}$ U C K Y

I have always been lucky. Always. I have pondered my ultimate good fortune, American, child of the fifties and sixties, accepted and admired, quick and easy, well-enough liked, traveled and intelligent, and raised by admirable parents. I have even insisted that my mistakes and failures have been filled with luck and good fortune. Every fall has opened a new door, luckily enough, and the adventures have multiplied and the scenarios have remained nearly implausible in their complexities and coincidences and uncanny timing.

Must be good luck. Turn around and spot a girl's lost contact lens at twenty yards on a New York City street, a chance glint of light on the pavement, just in time to save the day. Luck to have been at the right place at the right time, to meet the right person for the right future. Checks arrive in the mail just when the bills are due, and a lucky buyer calls just when the sale is nearly over. The doctor's report has some wrinkles in it, but the future remains solid, it'll all be fine, and turns out just so. Retirement arrives, and a day or two before wondering too heavily about the health insurance, a phone call offer of a new job, a new career, a lucky engagement.

Here's how lucky I am: friends in Shenandoah won two hundred and sixty million dollars. I never gave it much of a thought, but on an afternoon off, waiting in the doctor's office, mom-millionaire came in,

211

and we shared some old catching up, how's-the-daughter-doing kind of talk. The mom and husband, maybe the daughter too, had just bought matching sports cars, convertible BMWs. The nurses went out to look at Mom's new car, praises of appreciation. We talked on, and I never had reason to ask about the couple hundred millions they were juggling. I had some bills to pay, and American Express was creeping up in a troublesome way, but payday was coming, and my thoughts were in the hundreds of dollars, not millions. I believe I am very, very lucky.

CLOCK

During the day, time flies and busy-ness prevails, making time a filter and a valve, an announcement and a finish line. Time is the day's puzzle, a gadget and a goad. For most of my waking hours, I watch the time but disregard the clock. But my alarm clock, at bedside, is a ritual and a responsibility, night and morning. The clock is digital and has radio and a range of sounds, from ocean waves to jungle bird calls and rain. The clock also has two separate alarms, so that morning appointments are safe, even if one alarm fails to roust me from sleep. To get up and make the coffee, and to wake wife Betty, for work.

One alarm is typically set for five fifteen. The other for five sixteen. Radio alarm on the first, Bible preaching on a local station. The second alarm, set for one minute after the first as a sort of short snooze alarm, plays electronic choir sounds entwined with church bells, radio sounds. In an unusually slow start to any day, with no particular pressure on, the alarms are set for seven twenty-two and twenty-three, and I'll push the clock's snooze feature for an additional ten minutes' rest.

The alarm clock is the first greeting of the day, announcing the first responsibility of the day: getting Betty off to work. Setting the clock is also the day's final chore, releasing me to the time in between. Sleep. And rising, anxious or jolted out of dreams for whatever reason, I check the clock, doing the math on how much time remains, like an old man counting the possible years left. Sleep. Death. That I could be in such control of time.

$\mathcal{F}$ INALLY

I will say "Finally," as a sigh, in deep-down affection for life and ultimate rest from its cares. I care deeply for quiet moments and any chance to close my eyes without fear or anxious thoughts. I fall asleep too quickly each night and awake in the morning longing already for the coming evening, when the worries of the day will be past. I think my last word will be just that: "Finally," and perhaps just enough time, just enough presence of mind, to say "Thank you; thank you, Lord."

I have loved life, and loved each day, and my path has crossed so many others, and each crossing has been an adventure and a joy and a treasure. But I am tired. Not so much worn, but tired. I look forward to a new life, a joyous and certain new assignment, permanent, somewhere near to the entranceway of heaven, and I pray I will be assigned to assist at that gateway, dusting off feet, answering questions, pointing the way, and assuring glory closer to God for each new traveler at the gate.

On my tombstone: "Finally."

$\mathcal{T}$WO $\mathcal{P}$LACES—$\mathcal{T}$HREE

I am pulled between two places, always; perhaps three. I am pulled between wherever I am and all the places I've been, without real special regard for which one, whichever my mind rests upon for a moment, when I return to those places, times, faces, smells, tastes, sorrows, longings, successes, and happinesses. The tension between now and every other time is tangible, at times painful. The longing is real, though it doesn't require return or reliving an event or relationship; it's simply longing, for things already realized and lived.

The other place is an idealized place, and I have lived there all my life. The tension between here and now and this wonder of future or possible past is just as real as being drawn to a specific person or specific place from the past. The idealized resting place, the perfect evening, the comfort of unknown arms, the possibility of a choice not made, lost in the past or plausible in the future. I could tell you so much more about this pull, not fantasy, not imagination, but as real as this moment today. It pulls.

SOME PLACE

I come from Northfield, Minnesota; born in New York City, but raised in Northfield. Lived there three times: ages one, four to six, and junior high school. We moved so many times. We came from nowhere, but leaving Northfield in 1960, in teenage love with a beautiful girl, established Northfield as my hometown, where my heart resided, and it's been hard—impossible, really, to return there. I come from Minnesota.

I come from Pennsylvania. I went to high school at a Quaker boarding school in Bucks County and graduated from college in Allentown, married a girl from suburban Philadelphia, worked and lived in Allentown for seven years after living in New Jersey for four, and built a cabin in Potter County, near Coudersport. I come from Pennsylvania.

I come from New York City. I was born there. My mother's family came from New York City, and my brother still works in the city. I know the geography of New York and worked on lower Broadway after I dropped out of college my freshman year. In my later college years, I spent vacations working for Manpower, day labor, and have done every sort of job in the city. I drove to New York two or three nights a week for three years from work in New Jersey to do graduate study at TC, and I drove from Allentown regularly for a year to complete my doctoral study and dissertation. I come from New York City.

I come from Denmark, having lived there and worked there almost as a Dane, speaking and instructing in the language. I married into the country, and its values and systems run deep in my blood. I left for loneliness and returned only once, overcome with the loneliness of being there, but I come from Denmark.

I come from Wisconsin, where I escaped from Denmark, married, and found my true vocation chasing after teenagers with an assistant principal's walkie-talkie in my hand. I come from Wisconsin only because I found my life's calling there.

I come from Page County, Virginia, because it's where I have settled, first for reason of parents, then job, and finally family. I come from Page County, Virginia, because I have invested time and heart and have committed myself to the place and the people. I have children I call my own and a grandchild I call my own, and I pray they will return to Page County from their travels, as this is where I will be. I come from Page County, Virginia.

NOT ME

Black Dog has a cancer, a growth on the side of its upper jaw. Started small and has spread now, as if the dog had a big, long chew of tobacco in its mouth. Black Dog does not know it is dying, and it still wags its tail and barks when food or persons are on the way. Black Dog has been chained all its life, twenty-foot radius on the world, except when the chain breaks and it runs free, only to get its line tangled in the underbrush.

Two weeks ago the vet said Black Dog had a couple of weeks to live, maybe a month. The vet wanted to see the dog in ten days to two weeks, see if the medicine might shrink the cancer, maybe prolong life. The vet said that an operation would not help, that the cancer would come back and the operation would be painful and disturbing for all.

Black Dog is nearly twenty years old, one of a litter of mutt pups dealt out to friends by a high school teacher. Black Dog is female, and the children named her Honey Bear, but functionally she's been the black dog and in no way a Honey Bear. Black Dog, faithful guardian of the driveway, constant barker, wagging its tail, escaping from time to time, a chance to run. Its own world, small and understandable. Food. People. A chance to run.

MEETING IVORY ROSE— BASED ON A TRUE STORY, 2012

Everyone has a story to tell; it's just that some want to tell theirs more. But so few actually do. I met a lady who simply told her story: made up her mind to lay it all out and followed through. While some are too shy or ashamed to tell, many believe no one's interested, and most can't manage the chore, I met a lady who just went ahead, apparently without polish or fanfare or much expense, wrote her book. Saying, in effect, "There you go!"

But I'll bet there aren't many folks who, in quieter moments, wondering what a life is really worth, wouldn't want to tell their tale or spread some news, or finally get something off their chest. I'll bet there are more souls than we'd guess, just looking for a way to tell their story, even harboring a shamed dream to write the book. Or sing the song. Or paint a rich landscape of joys and sorrows and secrets and crimes. Victories and betrayals. A lifetime. Unfold surprises that parents or even grandchildren would never believe, catching their breaths. Tales mostly true, balancing acts real and imagined, perceived, cobbled together from bits and pieces gathered over years. Stories credible and accurate and true, at least from one side of the mirror.

But how and where to tell, and what if there were no audience? How to peddle even a small notebook half full? Selling private memories? And is this act of recording a tale really meant for an audience? Or is it simply naming a life? Transactions, gambles, treasures. I've dreamed since adolescence about writing a book but have never written much more than letters and reminders, lists of things to do, a few bursts of emotion on paper. College composition, and then a writing class or two with faint stabs at letting go, briefly forgetting to be embarrassed, sharing moments long since faded, silenced, and otherwise set aside. Or just lost.

I think about this every day now, maybe a symptom of age, of retirement, a narrowing of the field of adventure. Mostly, I think about telling pieces of my life's story while driving to and from work, an hour each way, conversations with myself about what I'd tell, who might listen, how much or how little I would have to hold back. I recently began to see the comedy in my commute to the college, seventy-five miles an hour in the car and then home again, hours a day, thinking, staring, sitting on the wheeled bench, hurtling through space. Speeding while time and life slip through my fingers.

And then one day, on Interstate 81, between Woodstock and Winchester, I met a lady who told her story. Let me tell you how I encountered her. A simple tale it is, free, yet priceless. And not a treasure to hide from prying eyes for fear of being stolen.

I met the lady on the way to work, and I wouldn't have noticed, except I was driving fast, as usual, and a tractor-trailer passed me in a blur of black and bright steel noise, going at least eighty or eighty-five, booming along. But as it passed, I caught a blink of a picture in the upper left corner of the rear doors on the trailer, a small mural, perhaps three feet wide by five feet high. It was a faded picture of a girl standing by the road and the blurred word *Dreams* angled at the top of the picture in childish script. Dreams, and a girl, maybe with a suitcase. Dreams. Why such a picture on a semitrailer? Surely not part of a trucking outfit. Too high up to be graffiti. I thought I could see another smudged word at the top of the picture: the rest of a title, like an old poster on a boarded-up movie theater. I remember it was a lonely picture, sad in every way. Something-or-other *Dreams*.

The truck was half a mile away before I decided that I wanted a closer look at the picture, and I figured I had plenty of time to catch up, at least ten miles to my exit at Middletown. I could still see the speeding truck clearly, fifteen or twenty cars and trucks between us, so I pressed the accelerator down and set my sights on the truck, the picture, and pulled onward. Toward *Dreams*. A few miles down the road, and I began to creep closer to the rear of the tractor-trailer. The picture came into clearer view, though it was weathered and dull. It was indeed a painted picture, not a poster; looked hand painted, perhaps by a teen. And the smudged word in front of Dreams was barely visible, faded, so I got out pen and a scrap of paper from my bag on the seat and wrote *Dreams*.

The picture was of a girl by the highway, holding a suitcase, standing in front of a building with a sign: TRUX. And then the word in front of *Dreams*. *Torn*. *Torn Dreams*. It looked like a book cover, and I could see what looked like a person's name across the bottom, in smaller letters, also childish script. Rose. Ivory Rose. I copied it all down. *Torn Dreams*, a book, I guess, by Ivory Rose. A woman's dream about a story to be told, a faded painting of a girl on a journey, alone. Perhaps in harm's way. Or just looking for adventure. Or making an escape. A girl hitchhiking at a truck stop. *Torn Dreams*, by Ivory Rose.

When I got to work, it was easy enough to search for the title and author. As quick as for anything else on the Internet, there it was, Amazon, a for-real book. Sure enough, by Ivory Rose. Cover art on the book nearly the same mural as on the tractor-trailer—a sign on a diner, USA TRUX, suitcase, lonely girl. And then, as clear as life and death, across the bottom of the of the book's cover, something more than was written on the truck: "Based on a True Story." *Based on a True Story*. Ivory Rose's story. I read several of Amazon's pages from inside the book, about a troubled home or marriage, an angry husband, a boyfriend, noticed some misspelled words, but stopped long enough to order a copy. Then, the real key to my life's writing puzzle: the ISBN, AuthorHouse publishing, and a note about the author. Ivory Rose, true name or not, was in fact a lady who simply chose to tell her story, based on truth and life and years. But I am certain based even more on a dream, a dream to tell her story.

I searched the net for the publisher, a cut-rate self-publishing outfit, packages ranging from several hundred to thousands of dollars. Ivory Rose may have taken the least costly route, which offered limited editing, proofing or professional cover art, straightforward printing on demand. But even so, Ivory Rose had put the copyrighted story of a life on Amazon, next to thrillers, how-to's, best sellers, and great American novels. *Torn Dreams*, ISBN and a price tag, fifteen dollars, two five-star reviews. My release from more than a half century of wondering and longing and holding back was immense, tangible, pure excitement. A life's story in print, regardless of editorial acceptance or publishing-house quality or quantity to sell. An artifact, evidence of a lifetime, in easy reach, affordable. Based on a true story.

Thank you, Ivory Rose, for saving a life. And a story.

Hoot: A Page County Story Retold

Hoot was the best big brother a child could ever want. I remember him like it was just yesterday, like he was still sitting in his chair in Mom's living room, watching the TV. He was like a second father, in his chair, telling us kids to be quiet. He was tired from work, and he wanted to watch his show on TV. Then he would turn and say, hey go clean out my pants pockets from all the sod dirt, they're on the porch, and you can have any change you find. We ran off, fought over who would get which pocket, and sure enough, there was always some change in there. And loads of dirt.

Hoot worked in sod, down the country, and he worked every day, hard, unless it rained of course. He was strong, and handsome, and always happy. He was wonderful. Everybody loved Hoot. Later on, when he got out of sod, Hoot worked at the chicken plant and always had packs of chewing gum in his pants pockets, and we could take a stick of gum if we hung up the pants. Neatly. Take them up to his room, upstairs. We loved Hoot, Maynard probably the most, he was three or four years old, the baby. Nancy was six, and I was just ten. Everybody loved Hoot.

I was ten when Hoot was killed. We cried and cried, and Maynard was just plain scared, not knowing what was going on, he was just a child; I can't say how much worse Mary or Eva or Greasy took it, they were older, and Daddy never said much about it at all. We didn't know how Hoot could be gone.

Hoot was twenty-five when he was killed, and it was just a freak accident, needless. But the worst was, they blamed it on Hoot, when it was really Trask Lucas who was driving. Tony Painter told me all about it, years after. Tony was friends with Trask, and Tony says Trask told him the truth about the accident, not too long before Trask was shot on the mountain. Killed. But Hoot's death was an accident like so many, somebody dies in a car wreck. Mom said it wasn't any reason to try to set the matter right, it was too late for Hoot anyway. I think Hoot was her favorite, her oldest boy, Dad's boy, Melvin Jr. In the old black-and-white pictures, Hoot looks just like Daddy at that age. Hoot. He was my favorite, forever.

I was ten. It was a Sunday afternoon, and Hoot drove down to the Hawksbill Diner to meet up with Squirrel Housden, who was going to drive with Hoot to take Hoot's girlfriend, Connie, down to Maryland. Connie worked in Maryland and visited in the County on weekends. Hoot said he loved her, but he couldn't see settling down just yet. I think he had other girlfriends, but I know he loved Connie. He said he did. Hoot and Squirrel would have fun driving down to Maryland and back, and Hoot decided to get something to eat while he waited for Squirrel, before they left to pick up Connie.

At the diner, Hoot put in his order for food, and then Trask Lucas and Jimmie Cage came in, laughing, cutting up. They had a car and wanted to show Hoot. He was going to eat, but they said come on anyway, you got to see this car, we'll just go for a spin. Hoot told the girl to go ahead and fix the food, that he'd be right back. Squirrel said later that if he had only shown up at the diner on time, he would have told Trask and Jimmie to get lost, that he and Hoot were getting ready to leave. To this day, Squirrel blames himself. If only he had gotten there in time. Tell Trask to get lost.

Hoot never got back to the diner. Squirrel met up with the rescue squad down the road and they told him two boys had gotten hurt, real bad, a car accident. Squirrel hung around. One of the injured boys told the squad that there were three of them, and they looked and found Hoot, thrown way far away from the rest, bad shape. Squirrel left in a hurry and drove out to Honeyville, told Mom that Hoot was in an accident, a car wreck, and the squad had taken him to the hospital. Mom and Dad drove to the hospital, and the town deputy, Dotson, told them they've already taken Hoot to Bradley's, the funeral home.

The story is that Hoot is driving. He is thrown from the car when it rolls. The other two boys get out of the wreck, and Jimmie crawls down in the ditch to get away. Maybe been drinking, or just scared. Trask gets out of the car by the time the squad arrives, and he's the one who tells them there was three in the car. The squad searches around and finds Hoot, twenty, thirty yards away, dead. So Trask and Jimmie hear that Hoot is dead and that's when they decide to say Hoot was driving, not Trask. They likely worked it out, Hoot had a car and a job and insurance and the wrecked car wasn't theirs, just borrowed for a spin.

No one believed the story, but who's to tell? Not even the fact that Trask's foot was hurt bad, they say a piece of his heel was torn off, stuck under the gas pedal. And Trask walked with a limp after that, until the day he was shot, a limping witness to his lie. And anyway, Trask told Tony Painter that he had been the one behind the wheel. I'm glad he told, because Jimmie Cage never talked about it until the day he died. But Trask told Tony, and Tony told me, and then Trask was shot on the mountain, killed. No one ever found who killed him. Mom said it served him right.

They drove Hoot's red convertible up to the house, and Mom had them pull it into the woods, under the trees, along the edge of the upper field, away from the house and the barns. It's still there today. Hoot's red Chevy convertible. 1961 Bel Air. From time to time, people see the car tucked away in the woods, the brush, and ask if they can buy it. Hoot's convertible. Mom says no. It's Hoot's car. Hoot. He was the best big brother a child could ever want. I remember him like it was just yesterday.

RETELLING "HOOT"

The story flowed off the tips of my fingers, across the keyboard, and onto paper. It became increasingly effortless as the several rewrites unfolded. It was creative journalistic reporting made easy by years of repetition of a simple yet compelling story, and refinement in telling and retelling. The essay reflected a story I had heard many times, told within the family. Hoot's formal black-and-white high school photograph occupies a prominent place in each of the Housden family homes, ours included. Likewise, Hoot is buried in a Housden family grave site, with his name, Melvin, chiseled in the headstone shared with father Melvin Sr., and mother, Calvin, years before his Dad's passing. Hoot's mom is still alive today.

My experience over twenty years living in Page County is that Hoot's death impacted each member of the family differently, some living out the more commonplace suffering and regret and longing, some brooding through bitterness, resentment, and alcohol, some maintaining a passionate and obstinate and destructive anger, pointless. The story of the accident is told often, mostly centering on the duplicity of Hoot's friends, in the fabricated explanation that Hoot had been the driver of the car the day they crashed, killing Hoot. Always the reminder that the actual driver had confided in others, admitting the truth, and the family knew.

The essay required nothing more than an appropriate voice, a simple recounting of the facts of the matter, and final justice. The essay would simply set the stage with the family's love for twenty-five-year old Hoot, relate the details of the day and the accident, settle the lingering doubt that Hoot had been driving the car, place the actual driver at the center of responsibility for the event, and tell how we know the truth. That the true driver later died in an unexplained, unsolved shooting on the mountain was simply to provide a mystery describing the full circle of justice. The repeated telling of the Hoot story never has included any conjecture on who did the killing, just that it happened "on the mountain," and that no one needed to know who shot him or why, just that he deserved it, serving justice in the end.

I chose the voice of a ten-year-old girl, a younger sister, but told as a ten-year old might do. When she tells the story, it contains only the information that a ten-year-old would find critical. Hoot was wonderful; Hoot worked in sod and at the chicken plant, and provided gum and change; Hoot was like a second Daddy; Hoot had his own chair in Mom's living room, as a parent would; Hoot warned and demanded, and the children paid him heed; Hoot had a girlfriend; Hoot ordered food at a diner on a Sunday afternoon, as a lone traveler might; Hoot was not the driver of the car; Hoot was the victim of a needless coward's lie; the children were shocked and saddened by his death; above all else, Hoot's memory is precious, and everybody loved Hoot.

The essay's voice includes grammar and inflection common to Page County, the particular subject-verb alignment, run-on thoughts, tense shifts, and descriptions not separated from dialogue. Additionally, the local points of reference and the geographical relationships, such as "in the County" or "down the country," figure significantly, as in a tale related by a child from Page County. I attempted to weave the simplicity of a child's telling of the story, the details, with a proud little sister's admiration, mild blame mingled with regret, and the undying memory.

Likewise, the details of the story flow from my own two decades' living in the County, the names and places and critical stopping points: the Hawksbill Diner, the squad, Honeyville, the mountain, and Bradley's Funeral Home. Writing "Hoot" required simply the distillation of a few important facts and locations, an attempt to describe an evening at home with the children, a few friendships and a tentative girlfriend relationship, ordering food at the diner, the wreck's aftermath, the deputy, Dad and Mom, and a memorial car pulled in under the trees to rust and rot—all true details, with the exception of several heart-wrenching changes of name.

Finally, and as critical as voice or story line, the real backbone of "Hoot" as creative journalism is the interplay of needless loss, duplicity, and eventual justice. Mother Housden always adds that there was nothing to do about it anyway, that in the end justice, was accomplished. To add that so many of Hoot's friends and family worked where the shooting took place—on the mountain—as did Melvin Sr., would simply cloud the telling of the story. A ten-year-old girl would not insert this potential moral complication into her story of admiration. Hoot was simply the best big brother a little girl could ever want. "Hoot."

BRIEF BIO AND FAREWELL

It's time to tie this together, end the book, offer a brief biographical sketch, and perhaps offer some closing comments about story patterns and threads and the fabric's weave. The book was arranged chronologically, though loosely, as it was never intended to be an autobiography or memoir. Each piece was written for its own sake, a brief burst of writing or an essay on something running deeper in the soul. Even so, you might want to have the quick rundown of *who* and *where* and *when*. Likewise, the value of these sketches, as I call them, is not in the individual pieces so much as in the threads of significance that run through them individually, or that weave them together in the entirety of a life. That will require another book. But for now, at least, here is a biographical recap in a few hundred words:

I was born in 1946 in New York City, and we moved several times in the first years, from the City to New Jersey, lived with my dad's parents, back to the City, and then to Northfield, Minnesota, where my father was chaplain at Carleton College. We were there for a year, and then my father returned to grad school at Columbia, in New York, and we lived in Shank's Village north of the City, a retired military base peopled by City students.

After a year or so, we were back in Northfield; Father was chaplain again, and I attended kindergarten and first grade there. Wonderful little farming and college town, could have been a great place to call a hometown, perhaps even home. After first grade, we moved east to Hamden, Connecticut, Father giving up academic life to manage a foundation. A year later we were in New Jersey, and Father taught at Teachers College, Columbia, and I attended third through sixth grades in Leonia. Then we were back on the road to Northfield, where Father was dean at Carleton.

Two years later, Father gave up administration and returned to teach at Columbia, staying there until he retired in the 1980s. My brother, Roger, and I went to co-ed Quaker boarding schools in Pennsylvania for our high school years, a special bonus offered to Teachers College faculty. My four years at George School were in many ways the best of my life. I went on to the University of North Carolina at Chapel Hill. Roger went to Antioch College, dropped out after two years, and became a Vietnam War conscientious objector.

I dropped out of UNC in March of my freshman year and was drafted, but got a temporary deferment when I failed my physical. I enrolled at Muhlenberg College before I was called up again, eventually graduated, and went into teaching in East Orange, New Jersey. I married Hollace Keay, who was one year behind me at Muhlenberg, and we lived in northern New Jersey for four years, both teaching full time. I entered graduate programs at Teachers College, where my father taught. I returned to teach at Muhlenberg College in the education department, and Holly and I separated. Holly died a year later, and I stayed on at Muhlenberg, teaching full time and working part time in local restaurants.

In 1976 I received a Muhlenberg faculty fellowship to study in Switzerland; I met Lisbeth Sølvhøj during the trip and we married in Denmark, in 1977. I returned to Muhlenberg College for a year, living in Allentown with Lisbeth and her daughter, Birgitte. We then left the States for Denmark, Lisbeth's dreams to settle in the United States come to naught. I taught English in Copenhagen and then went into restaurant work; I was a cook and then worked three years as *køkkenchef* at a restaurant in Tivoli Gardens. Lisbeth and I divorced in 1982, and I later moved to Jutland, Denmark's mainland, near Lisbeth's parents and sisters. I taught Danish language skills to Palestinian and Kurdish refugees with the Danish Refugee Commission in Hadsund, but after two years in Jutland left Denmark and returned to the United States, settling with friends in Milwaukee.

I met Angela Dentice, and we married. I taught as a substitute in the city high schools, became assistant principal and then principal. After four years, Angela and I divorced, and in 1992 I moved to Virginia, met and married Betty Jane Housden, and was principal at Page County High School in Shenandoah until I retired in 2008. I then became dean at Lord Fairfax Community College, an hour's drive from our home, retiring again in 2012 to part-time work at the community college center in Luray, near home, and began teaching online with Liberty University.

The book's sketches were written entirely at Lord Fairfax Community College, in four classes taught by Professor Brent Kendrick, one of my prized faculty. I write these few biographical notes a year following retirement from the deanship and note increased difficulty in my ability to easily recall the events of my life. The drive to complete the book comes from revisiting a compilation of the essays and being surprised by stories I can clearly recognize, but which I would not have easily recalled. I remember my father reporting some of the same kinds of things as he drew into old age, retired. This brings me to two of the threads and themes of a life worth living.

When I returned from Denmark on vacation from Tivoli, I asked my father how he was doing in retirement, what he was doing. He seemed ill at ease, bored, and anxious. My mother stayed busy with community service, but Father walked the country roads around Bridgewater, Virginia, and did little else except some strenuous yoga exercises in the morning. He had taught a course at James Madison University, volunteered in a local library, helped my mother with her welfare projects. Why not teach some more, write another book? Anything. He was disinterested in the ideas, lacking any spark. I did not understand at the time, but perhaps I do today. Powers and drive and initiative slip away, bit by bit, after the hard-driving daily working life. I feel today much of what he seemed to express in the early 1980s.

And what about the stories I've pulled together, arranged in something like a time line? What thread runs through the pictures drawn, what general or specific image might capture the life? I've read and re-read the better pieces and located what I think characterizes the essence of it all, and as a bonus, I believe it's also the essence of my father's life, adding emphasis to the thread, almost a generational blessing. Or curse.

The singular half sentence of a hundred pages and perhaps two lifetimes is this, in the *Last Stop* essay, arriving in Virginia from Milwaukee. I had stopped in Mount Jackson, only a half hour from my destination, called Mother and Father to say I'd see them the next day, and slept the night in a motel. I arranged to meet them at New Market Gap, on US Route 211, picking up my father on the roadside at the top of the mountain. He would walk a mile on the highway up the western side of the Page Valley and wait, and we would ride together in the truck, into my new life. My new life, like he had done so many times; like I had done so many times.

Here's the line, the first thread: ...*as I turned the truck and trailer back onto the road at the top of New Market Gap, my father leaning forward in the seat....* I can see him today, intent on the road ahead, full of hope and anxiety. That moment was *his* adventure, all over again. I can see him in my mind like it was yesterday. He wasn't even with me; he was starting something new, heading out, yet heading home. The first thread is simply that I am my father, unsettled and wandering, for years and years, until circumstance says it's the final move, the final nesting, solid, home.

For my father, it was twenty-five years in New York, at Teachers College. For me, it would be twenty-five years in Page County, almost all at Page County High School. And, of course, Betty to round out the picture. And that's where the other thread comes in. We attended church, and I had been reading in the Bible; one Sunday, she grabbed my hand and said, "Come on," and we stepped forward and gave confession and did the Baptist dedication.

Strangely enough, turning to that same *Last Stop* closing snapshot of my dad re-creating his own adventure through my retreat from Milwaukee to the mountains of the Blue Ridge, I find the other thread that weaves into firmer and warmer fabric as the years pass: *...I never would have guessed the turn toward God I was going to experience in Page County, the deep knowledge that He was riding with me and that He had never been far from my side, even as I ignored or dismissed or defied Him along the way. Maybe not my turn toward God. His turn toward me.* Threads, and a fabric, for another tale. Another Life. Another Story.

$\mathscr{E}$ PILOGUE — $\mathscr{G}$ ATHERING $\mathscr{F}$ LOWERS

And a book of remembrance was written before him for
them that feared the Lord.

MAL 3:16 KJV

My name was originally Scott Manning Phenix, in honor of my father's mother, Bessie Manning Phenix. John Manning was Bessie's father, and an enlarged photo of John gathering flowers on a solitary hillside in Ohio or Missouri or California hangs over our dining room table. I am captivated by the beauty of his moment on a hilltop. The photo speaks to me simply of generous old age, contemplation, and closeness to nature. The picture is my epilogue, rendering what I have taken to be that fitting end to gathering these stories I've told: a solitary and windswept hill, a life to ponder, and a bouquet of wildflowers.

John Manning died in 1918, a victim of the great flu epidemic. My parents changed my first and middle names from Scott Manning to Morgan Scott shortly after I was born, and I never received an explanation for the change when I asked, just that I was renamed to honor a close friend of the family, last name Morgan. But my brother's middle name remained the maternal grandmother's maiden name, Branscombe, and in recent years, I gleaned some fleeting, small clues about the Manning name and, much like this book's chapters, about what John Manning's picture on my wall doesn't tell.

There were, in fact, three people gathering flowers on the hillside, so the philosopher's lonely contemplation is gone. John Manning's daughters, Bessie and Ruth, were there. A separate photo, or one cropped from the original showing all three together on the same hillside, captures Bessie and older sister Ruth gathering flowers with their father; my brother Roger told me once that the flowers might have been for Ruth's wedding, and so would fix the photo to 1911. The girls look very happy, and in comparison with his daughters, John Manning now looks focused, strained, and worried. Unhappy, even.

The picture also rendered in my hopeful mind's eye an aging philosopher, a contemplative and gentle soul nearing the end of life, weighing what is important, what is not, perhaps drawing close to his Creator. Gathering flowers. But now I know he was not alone, that it was purposeful gathering, maybe even for a wedding. John Manning died seven years after the photo was taken, and therefore would have been sixty-five in the picture, much younger than the man in the picture appears to be, and younger than me as I think about the picture. Then—regarding the gentle contemplation—an anecdotal family obituary that my brother unearthed describes John Manning: "nervous; depressed spells; crying; afraid of going insane, but did not; criticized others much; kept whole family in turmoil." Perhaps I should have retained his name for good cause, seeing he was not a revered and aging ascetic, but simply a frail and ordinary man. Like me. And ordinary struggles. But there is more.

John Manning died and was spared a deeper family tragedy. I believe my parents timidly and unnecessarily weighed a potential for shame, before I ever imagined the question of the misdeeds that shadow our lives, misdeeds that blossom after our passing. In addition to the two girls, John Manning had two sons. One was "delicate, stayed at home, and pleased him." The family obituary tells that the other son, like the girls, "often tried him." Which son it was, the delicate one or the other, I do not know, but my father told of his own travel as a younger man to North Carolina to stand as family witness during the trial of one of those sons, for what were never described by family members with any more detail than the phrases "midnight walks" and "unspeakable crimes." The son died in a prison hospital in 1962. I believe that my name was changed for a never-spoken fear of shame.

In the unforgettable photo on the wall, I now see the flowers in John Manning's hand on that hillside as an awkward bouquet, wild colors turned to black and white, glad girls hidden from view, strain and worry and fear on a face older than its years, the old man's own unlikely death by mass tragedy sparing him a son's singular judgment.

An awkward bouquet. A gathering of too many pieces to hold comfortably in the hand. This is where I will leave my story, an awkward bouquet of tales and reflections and regrets, major turning points and fleeting, almost inconsequential snapshots. I gathered them in good faith and over good time. Like John Manning's picture on the wall, there are other stories and participants and events just out of view of my portrait. And finally, one never knows the years that remain, nor the revelations yet to come, nor the final judgment. Those go into another book.

Perhaps we all die in prison, in the end. I do believe, however, that we will be judged by the fleeting track we leave on the hillside, once we have gathered our flowers, whether for a treasured wedding or an undisclosed crime. And we forget that someone held the camera on that hillside. Likewise, I am convinced that nothing is hidden from the loving Creator's eye. I believe He too will gather us to Himself, in an awkward and loving bouquet.

Your Story: A Personal Letter

Dear Reader: My wonderfully patient and meticulous editor reminded me that part of my purpose in this book was to encourage others to write, and that the sentiment isn't always clear. She reminded me that the chance encounter with Ivory Rose only hints at how one writer can help another "by lighting the way."

I need to tell you that I spoke with Ivory Rose on the phone yesterday, to ask for permission to reprint her cover in my book. AuthorHouse had forwarded my request and Ivory Rose emailed me two days ago. On the phone, she was cordial, friendly, and said I could use the picture. She asked nothing in return. We spoke for ten or fifteen minutes, about how I had encountered her book cover on the back of a tractor trailer, about her follow-up volume to *Torn Dreams*, and about my plans.

I thanked her for the permission, of course. And then I thanked her for saving my life. She laughed, and I told her again that she had, in fact, saved my life. I had written the stories, but my grip on them was slipping, and my speeding drive to and from the college each day was becoming a dangerous blur. Until that day on the highway. Ivory Rose was an unexpected open door. An invitation to publish my life and my stories, pull things together. And live.

The worth of my Life is colored by time and by circumstance and by so many other persons; enhanced by the generosity of others; diminished by my own careless and selfish dreams. The worth of my Story is translated by limitations of skill and energy and persistence. But thankfully, I have been blessed with many years of life, and by the late coincidence of a remarkable professor and his passion for memoir and creative nonfiction. My encouragement to you is to embrace the time and capture the words which best describe your journey. The durable and coherent publication is within your reach. And thank you once again, Ivory Rose, for saving my Life. And my Story.

With kindest regards. Morgan Scott Phenix, October, 2013

250

Made in the USA
Columbia, SC
21 November 2023

26912393R00147